BI

forever

MARRIAGE

THE 5 PILLARS TO LIFELONG INTIMACY IN YOUR MARRIAGE

KING OF KINGS

Forever Marriage: The 5 Pillars to Lifelong Intimacy In Your Marriage

I would like to dedicate this book to my lovely wife, Rhonda. She has been a true soulmate and is an inspiration of what a Godly wife should be for so many young ladies. Being able to create a "forever marriage" with her is definitely a blessing from God.

I also want to dedicate this to all the married or soon-to-be married couples who want a forever marriage and for their marriages to thrive...

MARRIAGE COVENANT

1 CORINTHIANS 13

My love for my spouse is *patient and long-suffering*.
My love for my spouse is *kind*.
My love for my spouse *does not envy*.
My love for my spouse *does not parade itself*.
My love for my spouse *does not seek its own interests but theirs*.
My love for my spouse is *not provoked to anger or jealousy or envy*.
My love for my spouse *does not think on evil*.
My love for my spouse *does not rejoice in iniquity, but rejoices in the truth*.
My love for my spouse *bears all things*.
My love for my spouse *believes all things*.
My love for my spouse *hopes all things*.
My love for my spouse *endures all things*.
My love for my spouse ***never fails***.

And over all these virtues put on love, which binds them all together in perfect unity.

— COLOSSIANS 3:14

In this book you will hear me say a lot about a "Forever Marriage." If you're married, want to get married, or even if you don't think you ever will, it's important that we understand what marriage (or selfless relationships) are supposed to look like, and for what purpose God intended them.

But before we can really dive in, I must be clear. A forever marriage is NOT a marriage where you stay together until one or both of you dies. Staying in a miserable marriage and not getting a divorce is not what I consider a forever marriage.

Why would you want to be a roommate with your spouse for the rest of your life instead of experiencing an intimate and passionate marriage, where you can't wait to wake up each day to do life together?

That's what a forever marriage is. No matter what life throws at you or what you go through, you stick together, and your love for one another grows every day. You're excited to be with the other person. You look forward to talking with them and sharing your dreams with them and hearing theirs.

They are your best friend and closest ally. You can trust them with all of yourself; they are safe ground. You have their back no matter what. You'll die for them, and are willing to sacrifice anything and everything to protect them, provide for them, and love them.

A forever marriage is God's love in action. Two servants serving and loving the other as better (higher priority) than themselves. Selfishness does not exist. Offense does not take root, nor any slanderous or derogatory words.

Both spouses speak life, not death, into their marriage and over their partner. You're a team; dedicated to each one's unique God-given role and responsibility for the marriage to thrive. And why should your marriage thrive?

Because God ordained it from the beginning to take dominion and authority over all of His creation and to multiply. Multiplication is prosperous, not confining. When we're living a forever marriage we impact and influence those around us; displaying the light of Christ in us to a world full of darkness and selfishness.

When your gaze is fixed on God, nothing will derail you. Doesn't that sound like a blast? It is! And your marriage can experience this joy as well.

In this book I'll share with you the five pillars of a forever marriage that will fuel and empower you and your spouse to live the life you were destined and created for, and become the example for all marriages around you.

Are you ready?

Biff Adam
Marriage Counselor
Founder of Soulmates Ministries
Leader of Soul Mates at CFBC

1

FOREVER MARRIAGE

Forever Marriage.

What comes to mind when you hear those words? Do you think of Disney movies where the damsel in distress is rescued by an arrogant and self-righteous man who seems to have everything but needs a beautiful, smart, and endearing woman to complete his quest? But instead, she rescues him from himself and they live happily ever after?

What about Hallmark or the Lifetime Movie Network and all of the perfect endings you encounter there? Don't get me wrong. My wife loves those movies and for good reason. We all want love and happiness and security. Those movies paint the perfect picture of what relationships could and should look like. It's why we crave it so much, even if we aren't fans of Hallmark movies. (Can I get an amen!)

Or, perhaps when you hear forever marriage the first thought that comes to your mind is growing old with someone, retiring, and sitting together with warm blankets and hot chocolate on a wraparound porch out in the country, far away from worries and noise, just enjoying each other and nature.

Sounds nice, doesn't it? Who wouldn't love to escape it all, to sit in the middle of nowhere with no phone, no Internet, and no one calling you to complete an assignment or do the dishes?

Sign me up!

While growing older together or developing grey hair sounds nice, it's not what I mean by forever marriage. It's not just about growing old together or being married for several years and not getting divorced. It's not just that our marriages last or "survive" but how our thoughts, emotions, feelings, and commitments function throughout our marriages.

When you're as old as I am (my wife, Rhonda, never ages; she's still as beautiful as when I first met her in High School), it's not just about aging and long life. I've been blessed to be married to her for over 35 years now at the writing of this and it's been amazing what God has done with us through our marriage.

Every marriage has its ups and downs as change happens, but the one thing that stands the test of time is commitment to one another.

We know a lot of friends who have made it a long time in their marriages. As in, they've been married for many, many years. However, they lack the true life force of a forever marriage. Without intimacy, what do you have? Just an empty and dead cohabitation with someone you might loathe or feel you made a mistake marrying.

That's not a forever marriage, that's self-inflicted prison. And one each and every one of us has a choice to never experience, but this choice is every day. And when you do that, what sprouts is the most beautiful and powerful thing you could ever imagine.

Many marriages grow old together and then die, and they lacked the true essence of a forever marriage. A forever marriage is one where you may grow old together, thank God for that, and it also means that you can't imagine being without your spouse.

WHAT IF THEY WERE GONE?

Can you imagine a world without your spouse in it? If you're going through hard times right now, or perhaps you just had an argument this morning about money, in-laws, the kids, or when you're finally going to go on a family vacation again (it's been 20 years!), this may be easier to think about. You may even be relishing it and wishing it would come sooner.

With all kidding aside, marriage is a hard thing. It's not like it's portrayed in movies and TV or social media. It takes two people, who are completely committed to making it work no matter what, coming together and doing life as a team.

Marriage was created for unity and harmony. If you are going through a tough time right now or your spouse isn't loving you how you wish he would or your marriage could be better, you're in the right place.

But imagine for just one moment back to the day you got married. Do you remember how happy you were? Can you feel the fire in your belly the first time you kissed? The way you looked at each other and couldn't wait to see them?

Now take that memory and emotion and imagine if that were all gone. If you were on your wedding day, and suddenly, your spouse was hit by a car heading to the venue or the doctor called with shocking news that would rattle the entire marriage before it even got started.

How would that make you feel? That's what I mean by a forever marriage. That if you lost your spouse (whether through divorce or death) it would devastate you because of what they mean to you.

It's not that you can't live without them but that you don't want to.

IS A FOREVER MARRIAGE EVEN POSSIBLE?

One of our member's of our Soul Mates life group father passed away recently. He and his wife were married 42 years, and now that he's passed, she still speaks to him even though he's no longer physically present. And even the family had a fun laugh the other day reminiscing about him. That's a forever marriage.

Just two beautiful people loving each other unconditionally. It doesn't necessarily mean you finish each other's sentences, though that does tend to happen when you're with someone for an extended period of time.

Another one of our member's father says he still feels married to his wife even though she's been gone for over sixteen years. That's how much of a vital part of his life she played, and that's Biblical.

God tells us that a man and a woman become one flesh when they get married. They are no longer two individuals but one spirit. This is why divorce or death is so traumatizing for many people. Whether through death or by choice of separation and divorce, the pain is the same. We were meant to be together forever.

Now before we go any further, I want to be very clear. If you have a parent or a friend or you yourself had a spouse who died and you or they remarried, that doesn't mean you didn't have a forever marriage.

DEATH IS NOT THE END

I have a good friend who's wife passed away in her thirties and he remarried. One of the things his second wife said to him was, "I know how much you and your wife were like this and now she's gone. I don't know if I can ever fill that."

While she meant well, what he said in response shows us how we should love our spouses.

He used a great analogy in his response to her.

He said, "No, no, no. You have to understand that was a book written while she and I were married. Now that book is on the shelf because our earthly marriage is over. But you'll have to understand though, that occasionally, I may pick that book back off of the shelf and remember. Yes, I will enjoy the time she and I had together, but each book has a beginning, middle, and end. Now there's another book."

This is common. I think God takes great joy in seeing someone remarry when their spouse passes away and when someone doesn't remarry. It's a personal choice.

Fifteen years ago, Rhonda was diagnosed with cancer. I remember my son asking me, who was sixteen at the time, "Dad, is mom going to die?"

Now if you know my son, you understand that he's very conscientious and doesn't just ask things flippantly and he doesn't expect answers to be shallow either.

His question hit me to the core. I didn't have an answer for him. A father is supposed to protect his family, and in that moment, I felt powerless. The hard truth and reality was smacked right in front of my face. Cancer was serious. Many people have died from it and that was a very real possibility for us.

I just looked at him and said, "I don't know."

His next question shocked me. I wasn't prepared for it. "If she does, will you remarry?"

I had never thought about that if I'm honest. And I'm sure you've never thought about that either unless your spouse became ill suddenly, or had an accident and is in a coma, or passed away. Why would you think about it unless something traumatic takes place? And even then, I'm sure it's not much of a forethought in that moment.

But if you have kids, or even if you don't, it's something to take into consideration and potentially discuss with your spouse if one of you were to not be here anymore.

Since my son expected a real answer, I just said, "I'll need to get back to you on that. I don't know what I'd do. Right now, we need to focus on your mother and her getting well."

I did get back with him a few days. I'm a social person. I don't think I could honestly be alone the rest of my life if Rhonda passed away. However, I told him, "I don't think so. I just don't think I could ever remarry. No one would ever measure up to your mother and what she means to me."

NO PERFECT MARRIAGE

Here's the deal. Is Rhonda the perfect wife for everyone? Would she work for you? Probably not. That's what's so beautiful about a forever marriage; it's perfect ONLY for you. You're perfect for them and they for you.

Does it mean you married the wrong person if your marriage is suffering and you don't feel any love in it at this moment? No. It just means you've grown apart and aren't growing together with God's help.

This is what we're going to discuss over the next five chapters. I've broken down what a forever marriage looks like into five key pillars for success and lifeline intimacy. We'll take each one and see what the Bible says about it so we use it as our guide and control for what a marriage is supposed to be. From there, we'll examine some practical applications to either restore our marriage or take it to the next level to achieve this forever marriage.

THE WORLD IS NOT YOUR MODEL

When I first started writing this book and teaching this series in our Soul Mates life group, we had roughly forty-three couples in the class. We got this number by considering how many couples attended church at least three times every four weeks.

That's at least forty-three marriages that the devil wants to destroy. According to the latest polls, the world would say that only twenty-one of those would make it, the other half would divorce.

Do you know what would be really cool to see instead? What if twenty years went by and we all met up again to reconnect and share stories of what's gone on during that time. And what if all forty-three of the members in the class were still married, and not just still together, but thriving. How cool would that be!

That's what God has for each and every one of you. God designed marriage to succeed, not to fail. He created a man and a woman to serve each other with selfless love as Christ loved the church and laid down His life for her. Everything God creates flourishes and accomplishes what He created it to do.

While the world says the divorce rate is 50% for both marriages inside and outside of the church, God says it's 100% when you do it His way.

HOW DOES GOD FEEL ABOUT DIVORCE?

God's plan is for marriages to last forever. In Malachi 2:16, He says, "'For I hate divorce!" says the Lord, the God of Israel. "To divorce your wife is to overwhelm her with cruelty," says the Lord of Heaven's Armies. "So guard your heart; do not be unfaithful to your wife.'" God says He hates it. He doesn't just sort of not like it or think it's okay, or kind of wish you'd say married, He abhors it. When you marry, He expects you to stay married. The scriptures show us early on what God's intentions were for male and female in marriage and how it's supposed to be a unified bond.

"Therefore a man shall leave his father and his mother and hold fast to his wife and they shall become one flesh.[1]"

It's pretty clear here what God thinks about marriages. He sees it as two people becoming one. It's kind of hard to divide a person into two without doing irreparable damage, right? Just imagine trying to split your body in half and expecting it to live, let alone thrive. Not possible.

What I find even more interesting is where God says this. Where is the book of Genesis located in the Bible? The beginning, right? And not just that, in chapter 1 God shares how He created all creation, and what does He share right after that? You guessed it! Marriage.

Right from the get go God sets his agenda and plan for us. This is the beginning of all creation and He says that a man and woman become one, then leave their parents, their childhood home, and do life together and create their own.

Before you shout for joy if you have in-laws you can't stand (or they can't stand you), this does not mean to abandon your parents. It just means you're no longer under their authority and hierarchy. You've now started your own family tree under God's authority. Your team is now you and your spouse, that's it. That's the way God meant for it to be.

MARRIAGE IS A BLOOD COVENANT

Jesus taught his disciples, and us by default, how we should approach marriage. He said in Matthew 19, "Haven't you read the Scriptures?" Jesus replied. "They record that from the beginning 'God made them male and female.'" And He said, "'This explains why a man leaves his father and mother and is joined to his wife, and the two are united into one.' Since they are no longer two but one, let no one split apart what God has joined together.[2]"

Many of you probably had that same scripture in your wedding vows or in your wedding ceremony. If I were to give you an apple and asked you to split it in two with your hands, could you do it?

For most, this would prove quite difficult. But what if I gave you a knife, could you do it then? All of you could, right? That's what the devil wants to do to every marriage. He hands each spouse a knife that can shatter their marriage if they use it.

But even if a marriage fails, each person is still incomplete. They've lost part of themselves in that loss because it's pretty hart to split something in half and it stay the same. Even the apple, when cut in half, is no longer a whole apple, it's two halves. It's the same with marriage.

Now the problem that causes this fracture is selfishness. We're selfish and self-preserving by nature. No one has to teach a child to say, "mine" or how not to share. On the contrary, we have to teach children gratitude, kindness, gentleness, and self control.

Some of us may be more selfish than others, and there are definitely seasons when it's easier to be prone to selfish tendencies. Where one person may struggle with one form of selfishness, another may struggle somewhere else.

WE MUST TAME OUR ALPHA COMPLEX

Rhonda and I used to have a Great Dane. Daisy was a great dog! If you know Great Danes, you know they're called great for a reason. They're huge! And Daisy was even bigger, even for a Dane. She weighed thirty pounds more than Rhonda. I'm not exaggerating. She really did. When we got her as a puppy, she was already big. We had seen her parents and they were both behemoths, so we knew she would be too.

While Daisy was easier to handle when she was a puppy, we knew there would come a day when things would become a lot less organized and calm to say it lightly. So, we did what every well-informed person does, we searched YouTube videos for how to raise a Great Dane and what to expect when they evolve into giants. The first videos were not promising and certainly did not leave us with warm, fuzzy feelings.

They were all videos of people talking about how they left home and came back to find their sofa gone. Literally gone. Obliterated! All that remained were remnants of what the sofa was made of.

Rhonda had looked at me and said, "If we're going to have this dog, we need to train her."

Since YouTube wasn't helping and only gave us more anxiety, we did what we should have from the beginning. We found us a dog whisperer. The first thing he did when he started training Daisy was train us by teaching us how to remove Daisy's alpha complex.

He said, "Your job is to make the dog understand where it lies in the hierarchy and where it falls in the house."

We learned that it's a German method to train big dogs. Apparently, big dogs wake up with an alpha mentality. They just naturally wake up every day thinking they're alpha and can run the show. The trick, this guy said, is to teach the dog its place.

He said he would show us what to do for free. It wasn't free by the way. He said, "If your dog is 30 or 40 pounds, here's what you do. When you wake up, go grab the dog around her four legs and pick her up. Hold her to your chest where her four legs dangle. The dog will probably start squirming to try and break free. Keep holding on until she stops fighting and goes limp. When you feel this, she's submitting. It's her saying, 'Okay, you're the bigger, stronger, better alpha than me, and I'll submit to you.'"

This all sounded lovely and all, but Daisy wasn't thirty pounds. She was a hundred and forty! Now, I'm pretty strong but that's a lot of weight to lift up and hold still while she squirms trying to break free. He went on to explain a few other things we could do to tame Daisy's alpha complex and exert our dominance over her.

We are the same way.

We wake up every morning thinking about ourselves. It's all about me. What are you doing for me? It's all about our needs. I can assure you, if you're reading this right now and you had an argument or some form of conflict with your spouse, you're probably using phrases like "I deserve" or "he treated me" or "made me feel." It's natural. It's always about me if we don't control it.

MARRIAGE IS WORK

It's our nature to be selfish and seek self-preservation. However, that's a root of selfishness. Remember, God said the two become one. Building a forever marriage is not easy, it takes work. It's something that is easy to give up on, but not easy to continue when things get rough or less than ideal for our selfish sides.

Like anything in life worth having, it takes consistent work for it to flourish. I'm not saying your marriage is like a dog, but there are some great comparisons using our dog Daisy as the example.

With her, one thing she absolutely loved was eating. Big surprise, right? She had a lot of mass she needed to sustain. We fed her twice a day. A lot, but twice a day. We'd tell her to sit in the foyer on this rug we had, and she'd go sit down. We'd tell her to stay, and would place her food by the back door in the kitchen. She would see it and her mouth would salivate, her tail would wag. You could tell she wanted to leap for it the moment the bag opened, but we told her to "stay."

Next, we'd spend the next five or so minutes doing something completely irrelevant to the dog food. We'd clean dishes, chat, fold laundry, whatever we had to do after dinner, and she'd just sit there. We did this every time she ate to train her we were the bosses and she had to obey us, or she wouldn't eat. We were taming her alpha complex.

If we had been lax some days and not consistent, it wouldn't have worked. Everything in our house would have become a dog toy and looked like a tornado had swept through.

Children are the same way. Now, I'm not saying you place your child on a rug and tell them to "stay" and force them to sit to eat dinner, but there is truth in this for good parenting.

Every child psychologist will tell new parents that consistency is everything. Without it, a child doesn't know how to behave. That's why parents have to teach them through routine, structure, and organization.

Now, there are thousands of different people reading this book right now. And every single one of them will have a different parenting style. But every one of them that wants to succeed will have consistency in that form of parenting.

If you discipline your child for something today but don't tomorrow, he becomes confused. He doesn't know which way to act and how consequences work for his actions.

DISCIPLINE IS CONSISTENCY IN ACTION

The discipline of consistency is key in life. At work, if you do something one day and then you choose not to do it the next day, you can't even know whether it works. While working on your marriage, consistency is everything.

You have to work constantly, consistently. Some days are going to be easier than others. Hopefully today, you have a receptive heart because today's an easy day. Hopefully, you're just so in love with your spouse and you go, "Oh, this is great, honey. We're going to build this forever marriage." That's great, but you know what? Tomorrow is probably going to be different.

The flip side to that is if today is one of those days you go, "Man, I'm glad we're reading this because I don't know what to do. Today is rough." For you, tomorrow will probably be a much better day.

Some days are easier than others. Building a forever marriage sounds like a fairy tale or a fantasy. Some days it'll feel that way and others will feel like a nightmare. The payoff, however, is the best thing for those who press onward and don't lose heart.

There are some pillars we can follow to equip us with the tools and knowledge to create our forever marriage with our spouses. These act as road guards to keep us on track and reveal where we've slipped and need to course correct. These pillars will serve as our reminders to keep us cultivating a forever marriage.

I want to make note, these pillars are not optional. They're required. They are iron clad rules you must follow if you want to have a forever marriage.

THE 5 PILLARS OF A FOREVER MARRIAGE

Honesty — Honesty is paramount in marriage. There can be no white lies or secrets in a marriage. This doesn't mean that if your wife asks you, "Honey, how does this dress look on me?" that you tell her it's great if there's another color that might make her look more flattering.

Honesty is not the best policy when you deal with emotions, but it's the *only* policy when you're creating a forever marriage. We will go deeper into how you express your honesty as there is a fine line between being coarse and rude and telling the truth in love.

If you want a forever marriage, you must have honesty (transparency) in your marriage.

Unselfishness — When it comes to your spouse, you cannot have unselfishness. You must put their needs before your own. You can't roll your eyes when their need does not fit your own agenda.

Unselfishness is a big deal for us because we're selfish by nature. That's why I say these are reminders because we have to think about them every day. Every day we must wake up and tame all alpha, and remind ourselves, it's about them not us.

Spirituality — the divorce rate in the church is the same as outside of the church. Going to church isn't spirituality. However, I do think it's very difficult to be spiritual and not go to church. However, it's easy to go to church and not be spiritual.

I use the word spirituality because I don't want to say religious. But I'm also careful when I say spiritual because I don't want to say, "Hey, if you're Hindu, you'll probably have a forever marriage." A forever marriage only comes by committing to Christ's ways.

If your life is pleasing to God, your marriage is going to be awesome. God does not desire for you to not have a happy marriage. It's the opposite. Spirituality is a big component to making that happen.

Team — The team approach means that you and your spouse have each other's back. It's you against the world. Here's the thing for you ladies, your children are not part of the team. I know that sounds really tough, but it's true. You can be the best godly parent in the world and realize that your marriage team is just you and your spouse.

So many marriages are damaged, and many beyond repair, because of the maternal instinct that pulls women toward their children before their husbands. That is not God's plan. That is also not scriptural.

We are going to look at this in greater detail so we know with certainty what is the best path.

The team in a marriage is the husband and the wife. And for you guys, work and your buddies is not part of your team. Nor is your favorite sports team or golf or hunting or fishing or anything that comes before your spouse. It's your spouse, and that's it.

Contentment — Contentment is the key to a forever marriage. This doesn't mean that you can't have any goals or pursue growth, development, and achievements. It means that whatever the future may hold for you and your spouse, that you are content with them only. You are pleased with them. You are joyful because they are your spouse.

MARRIAGE IS THE ANCHOR IN THE STORM

Rhonda and I don't have any secrets between us. Years ago I had an issue at work that affected our finances. Because I am self-employed, we've had times where we were extremely financially blessed and others not so much. This was one of the latter.

I was going through a rough time in business. I was trying to juggle everything and keep everything afloat at the same time. I came home one day, went into our bedroom, and just collapsed on the recliner. Have you ever had one of those days where you're just done? You're fed up with the world, with people, and with whatever is going on in your life? That's how I was feeling that day.

When Rhonda walked in, she immediately noticed my demeanor.

She asked, "What's wrong?"

Everything in me wanted to lock down and not tell her. I was supposed to be the provider of the family. I was supposed to protect her. And in that moment, I felt like a failure.

I took a breath and just let go.

I said, "Honey, I need to tell where we stand with our finances. Things are really tough right now. I just made a move with the broker-dealer that didn't go so well."

She said, "What is getting you down so much?" "I don't want to let you down."

At the time, we had had our lake house for about five or so years and we primarily bought it for our children and for their children as a place for us to retreat to and enjoy and relax. That lake house was everything to us and was a special gift for the children.

So I told her, "I'm scared that if something happens, I'll have the sell the lake house. I need to know how you feel about that if we have to do that."

"If we have to sell the lake house, we sell it." I decided to go a little deeper.

"What happens if things bottom out and we have to sell the home we're in now?"

"Then we sell the home we're in now," she said. She added, "Whatever it is, and whatever happens, I'm with you."

I don't know about you, but I can't think of something more amazing than having someone who has your back no matter what. In that moment, the weight that had been suffocating me stressing me out for days, was lifted off my shoulders all because she said she was with me no matter what.

She was content with whatever happened and wherever we had to go so long as we were together. That's what true contentment is.

Just think, how would the world look if every spouse was doing everything in their power to make their marriage the greatest marriage possible, and at the same time, each spouse was also content with whatever happened in that marriage, because they had their spouse?

Wouldn't that be amazing? That's what we're going to be studying in this book. Each chapter will close with *Love Actions* to implement in your marriage. These are things to consider and things you can do to show your spouse you love them and to create an atmosphere of selflessness. When you do them, your spouse will feel cherished and adored and your marriage will thrive, even if it's not right now.

PRAYER

Father, thank you so much for today. Thank you for every person reading these words right now. They are a blessing to Rhonda and me to be able to share your love and what you've taught us over the years with them so that they can have a forever marriage.

I ask that you bless each one of their marriages. I pray that every person reading this book will have a forever marriage. Not just one that lasts for a long time, but one that in their hearts, they know is a forever marriage.

Help us to love each other as we're supposed to, using You as our example. Thank you for those who found this book and are reading it and committing to making their marriage the best marriage possible.

We love you, Father, and pray these things in Jesus' name. Amen.

FOREVER MARRIAGE RECAP

- A forever marriage is not staying married to someone for a long time. A forever marriage is wanting to stay married to someone for a long time.
- The 5 *Pillars of a Forever Marriage* are honesty, team, contentment, spirituality, and unselfishness.
- You must put all ego and pride aside to have a forever marriage.
- Feelings and emotions are by-products of love in action.

LOVE IN ACTION

- What does a forever marriage look like to you?
- What are five things you could do today to let your spouse see and experience that they are number one in your life?
- Is there anything or anyone that you've placed above your spouse?
- Do you want your marriage to be a forever marriage?

- Are you willing to do whatever it takes to make your marriage a forever marriage?

---

1. Genesis 2:24 ESV
2. Matthew 19:4-6 NLT

2

HONESTY

A vital key to having a forever marriage is honesty.

It's not just required in a marriage, but it's also missing from American society today. Honesty is an unusual trait unfortunately.

I'm in the Financial Services business, which the government regulates with stringent guidelines. There are numerous steps of oversight we must navigate to ensure we're being trustworthy, honest, and acting with full integrity. They actually police it to prevent any attempt at fraud. And for good reason.

Out of my over thirty-five years in the industry and the thousand or so people I know, there's one gentleman I won't forget. His name is Michael Woodard. Michael is a great guy and I love him like a brother.

But one day Michael came to my office and he said something that has stuck with me all of these years, through the thousands of people and cases I've served. He said, "You know, Biff. Out of all of the people I know in this industry, you're the only one I trust."

Michael has said this on many occasions and it's always hit me hard in the gut. Was there really no one else he trusted? Why did he trust me and no one else?

Now, this may sound self-serving, but it got me wondering. Why aren't more people more trustworthy? And among the thousands of industries out there, financial services should be one of the most dependable. After all, you're trusting someone with your money and future. You better trust them!

But the truth is, oftentimes, people go blindly into contracts, deals, plans, friendships, relationships, partnerships, and marriage without a solid foundation on trust.

This is exactly where society has fallen today. People's word doesn't mean anything these days like it did in the days when a handshake was as good as a signed contract. Today, you better not make a deal unless it's in writing. And even then, you better have a good lawyer and underwriter to ensure you're protected. It's a shame.

THE STATE OF SOCIETY

The USA Today did a study where they polled 5,000 college students. They asked each one of them a series of questions as it pertained to integrity and honesty.

You'll be surprised at what their responses were. The first question was, "How many of you were taught honesty by your parents?"

Just over half of them (56%) said they were. They went on to elaborate that each one was taught about the importance of being honest and telling the truth. Only 56%! That's not very good. But it gets worse.

Then they asked the students, "How many of you would cheat on an important test?"

65% of them said they would cheat on a test if it was important.

It's interesting that they used the term "important" since that is subjective. What's important to one may not be to another. Or, what's important to you is actually something that was imposed or conditioned for you to think and believe by someone else, society, or a culture.

Even the very act of cheating could be seen as subjective. I mean, you know. If it's important, I guess I'll cheat to ensure I get a good grade or achieve the result I want. Right? And conversely, if it's not vital, I guess I'll tell the truth.

What kind of backward thinking is that? Where did we go wrong? And what's even more interesting to me is the fact that these were the numbers of those who actually were *honest* in their responses to the survey. I wonder how many of the 5,000 students who were surveyed actually would (or possibly have) cheated on a test, but weren't honest with their response. I imagine there were much more than just 65% who would cheat or lie whether on a test, on a resume, in a job interview, or in life if it meant gaining something or preventing a negative outcome.

SMALL LIES DIG BIG HOLES

How often do we do this in our marriages? It starts with what we consider a small lie, and before we know it, nothing but lies or half-truths come out of our mouths. We just dig our own graves.

In the same study, 36% said they'd lie for a friend who committed a crime. And 5% said they would steal from their parents if given the opportunity. The scary truth here is the "if given the chance" they would steal. As if they are just waiting for the opportune time to steal for their personal gain.

And just like before, only 5% claimed they would, but how many more have or would steal from their parents that actually didn't fess up in this anonymous poll? If 65% claimed they'd cheat and 36% claimed they'd lie for a friend who committed a crime, I'd wager the number is much higher than 5% for those who would steal from their own family.

This is a shame, but shows just how far our society has fallen. One of the best quotes I've heard about honesty, and it relates perfectly with this poll, is "Some are honest because they have never had the opportunity to be dishonest."

Someone might say, "I've never cheated on my taxes." But they're also a W-2 employee and can't cheat on their taxes since their employer must file their numbers to the IRS, and taxes are usually automatically withdrawn from paychecks.

I say this to make a point, but honesty and integrity is much deeper than merely lying.

INTEGRITY IS IN YOUR WORD

My grandfather had the highest integrity of any person I've ever known. I learned a lot from him as a young boy and even as an adult about what it meant to be full of integrity and to live by your word.

A man's word was his bond.

He owned a homestead, which meant he owned his land, house, and his business. He was a builder and had the oldest sawmill in the area.

One day my grandfather went into the bank for a business loan. Mind you, this was before banks actually did real banking like we see today.

So he goes in and tells the banker, "I need a loan."

The banker asks him, "What do you need a business loan for?" "To expand my business and make repairs," my grandfather said.

"Well, do you have any collateral?" the banker asked him.

Something you should know about my grandfather is that he's street smart, but not book smart. He only had an eighth grade education. And so, he didn't know what the banker meant by collateral.

And he said as much, "I don't know what you mean by collateral."

"You don't know what collateral is? It's something you own. When a bank makes a loan, they need something to hold as collateral.

That way, if you don't pay the loan back, they can actually take ownership of that property or whatever you listed as collateral."

"Well, I've got my home," my grandfather said. "You own the deed of your home?"

"Yes."

"Oh, well, just bring the deed as collateral. We'll keep the deed here until you pay off the loan, that way it covers us," the banker said. So my grandfather signed the Statement of Collateral (he didn't actually have to bring up the deed itself) for the loan. It was for a small amount, like $1,000. Now remember, this was back in the 40s, so a thousand dollars was a lot of money. That would be equivalent to

$18,326.50 in 2019[1]. Still not too much comparatively, but you have to also keep in mind, his home at the time was worth $40,000, which would be $733,060[2]. That's quite a bit of money on the line!

So, if my grandfather couldn't pay back the $1,000 loan, he was liable to not just lose his home, but his entire livelihood. But he signed the agreement and took the loan. As time passed, the loan eventually matured (came time for him to pay it back) and my grandfather went into the bank on the day the loan was due.

He walked in, took out the deed to his home, and placed it on the desk of the banker. He asked the banker when he, his wife, and his children had to move out of the house.

The banker was confused. "What are you talking about?" he asked my grandfather.

"Well, you told me that if I couldn't pay the loan off, and since I used the house a collateral, that I'd have to give you the house."

The banker held up his hands emphatically.

"Hold up! We don't want your house," he told my grandfather.

And he looked at him and asked, "How much can you pay?" "I have about $800," my grandfather said.

"Can you pay interest for a year?" the banker asked. "Yeah."

"Well, then we'll renew your note. When can you pay it off?"

"I can probably pay it off in the next month or two. I just can't pay it all off right now, so I'm here to give you my house since I can't pay," my grandfather said.

The banker smiled, but understood what my grandfather was getting at. You see, when you don't know, you just don't know. But even so, my grandfather only knew integrity. He had given his word.

But the banker stood and said, "Just pay us what you can today, and we'll renew a new loan for the difference. And you can pay that back when you're able to."

And so, they signed a new contract and my grandfather paid off the remaining balance of the loan the next month.

THE PRINCIPLE OF INTEGRITY

My grandfather was willing to give up his home and his family's entire livelihood because he had given his word that if he couldn't pay back the loan by a certain date, that he'd hand it over to the bank. My grandfather did life just like this. And right before he died, he told me that one of the biggest disappointments he had with how society had evolved was that you couldn't do business on a handshake anymore. People's word didn't mean anything.

That's the root problem we must address before we look into creating a forever marriage. Marriage is about honesty and integrity for two people, individually and collectively. Each person is their own individual who both have human traits like selfishness and self-preservation.

Honesty is vital for any marriage to thrive. Without it, what do you have?

There's a common phrase people say, "Love is all you need" but that's not true. That sounds good maybe when you're first getting married, or during your honeymoon, and even the first few years of marriage, but it's not accurate.

Any couple who has been together longer than a year (definitely 10 years) can testify to that notion. You need much more than love for a marriage to survive, let alone thrive. Marriage is hard, but it's also one of the most beautiful and powerful things you could experience, next to having children. But that's a different topic for another book.

Our human nature is selfish. The reality is that married couples are going to be selfish and seek to preserve their own interests. It's a survival instinct. If we want to preserve and protect our marriage, and have one that prospers, then we need integrity.

But before our marriages can have integrity, we ourselves must be a man or a woman of integrity. And go about our day-to-day lives with honesty and truth.

Theodore Roosevelt is another good example of this. He was a man's man. I heard a story about how he once beat up a cowboy in a bar because he was standing up for a woman's virtue. That's just the kind of guy Roosevelt was. He was a guy's guy and would take off his shirt for a stranger in a heart beat.

He also owned a large ranch called Elkhorn Ranch in North Dakota. And back in those days the cattle roamed around in what's known as *open range*. There weren't any fences or ranches like there are today. It was more of an honor system, where if you saw another cow or bull with someone else's brand on it, you just let them feed on your land or brought them back to the owner.

Well, one day Teddy and his top range hand were out on the land, herding the cattle. His name was Brian Catalan. On the first night, they were close to another rancher's land. And this man was not a friendly man to say the least. He was ruthless.

And Roosevelt and his ranch hand found a cow that was on their land, but it was covered under the seal (brand) of the other guy. Roosevelt's ranch hand said, "Don't worry. I can change the branding to yours. He's taken some of our cattle in the past. We can alter his brand and make it look like yours. No one will know. Besides, we're just getting back what's rightfully ours anyway. I'll do it tonight while we're branding the other cows by the campfire."

The next morning, Teddy Roosevelt said to the ranch hand, "We're headed back. When we get home, pack up your things. You no longer work for me."

The guy tried to argue and justify why he was willing to rebrand the cows when Roosevelt told him why he was letting him go.

He said, "You don't understand. I'm just saying it evens things out. He's probably taking ours, we're just getting them back."

But Roosevelt said, "It doesn't matter; that's dishonest. And someone who is willing to steal *for* me is willing to steal *from* me. I won't have either."

And sure enough, when they got back, the ranch hand packed up his things and left. I love this story of Roosevelt and it also shows why so many people loved him.

I've tried to teach my kids the same truths and principles about integrity. To me, the definition of integrity is doing what's right because it's right. Not because you get rewarded for it (sometimes you may even get punished or slandered for it), or not because someone found out about it, but just because it's the right thing to do.

DARKNESS IS A FALSE CAMOUFLAGE

What do you do in the dark? What do you do when no one is watching? What do you do when no one will think any less or different of you, because they don't know what you did?

I used to have my kids go rake the neighbors' yards when they were out of town. I did this to not only teach them to do unto others and to protect and look after the orphans and the widows[3], but to develop their integrity and work ethic. Integrity isn't always not lying or telling the truth. It's also doing the right thing and not expecting anything in return, or seeking recognition. That's why I had them tend to the yards when the neighbors were out of town so no one would know who did it.

But why was that the right thing to do? Where do we learn our morals and beliefs? What becomes our defining guide post to follow in life? For my family and me, this is the Bible; God's word.

Many don't believe in God, and instead, believe in the "universe" or nothing at all. And while I want to respect each person's personal beliefs, that just doesn't work. Without a definite and separate higher being, right and wrong is subjective. Then we fall into the new notion these days of "my truth is my truth, and your truth is yours."

No! That doesn't work and never will. If that were true, then why are murderers and rapist in prison? Why did we go to war against Hitler when he was killing hundreds of thousands of Jews?

If his truth was his, even though it differed from many others, then why did we classify him as "wrong" and go to war to stop it?

You see, that doesn't work. Subjective truth never works and just isn't logical. There's a reason why most everyone, no matter their background or culture in the world, all unanimously agree that certain things are right and certain things are wrong.

Why is that? Well, according to God's word, He's written His law on our hearts[4] meaning, God's moral compass and righteousness were prewired and preprogramed into each and every one of us. That is why we can all collectively agree with what it right and wrong despite our backgrounds, cultures, and spiritual beliefs.

Now, this is also changing in today's world as people are falling further into darkness and away from God. And now "there is a way that seems right to a man, but its end is the way of death.[5]"

We all need a standard. And scripture teaches us honesty and integrity as God sees it and originally designed it. Paul tells us in Ephesians 4:25 that we should put away lying and speak truth to our neighbor [other people] because we're all members of the same body [that is Christ's body if you're a believer][6].

Telling the truth or lying always begins with small things. It may start with telling a small, "white lie" that we believe is innocent, but once you do something the first time, it's easier to do it again, and then again.

We're supposed to speak the truth to one another and render judgements [declarations or utterances] that are truthful, just, and lead to peace[7]. But why does it matter? Why should we still be honest when no one is watching, or when it doesn't hurt anyone?

God tells us that "lying lips are an abomination to the Lord, but those who act faithfully [truthfully] are his delight.[8]"

A similar saying is "if a tree falls down in the forest and no one is around to hear it, does it make a sound?" Many will use this as justification for their lack of honesty or integrity. But God also tells us that *no creature is hidden from His sight, but all are naked and exposed to the eyes of Him to whom we must give an account.[9]"*

This all corresponds to how we are as individuals. And if we're willing to make excuses or justifications for integrity slip ups as it benefits us when we're single or when no one is looking, then we'll also do it when we're in a group, when it matters, when someone is looking, and when we're in a relationship.

This leads to disaster. We want to nip that before we even begin so your marriage starts on solid ground.

HONESTY IS A HABIT

Honesty all starts with your mind. What are the thoughts that you have every single day about others around you? What thoughts do you have about your spouse? What thoughts do you have about yourself? Honesty is more than what you say and what you do, it's also what you think.

Because "for as he thinks in his heart, so *is* he.[10]"

So what does being honest in a marriage look like? If it's so important and critical to the success of a marriage and any relationship, what are some of the rules for it?

If it's more than just doing what is right and saying what is right, but a habitual practice that we do every single day with our spouses, children, friends, family, and the workplace, what does that look like? There are six rules regarding honesty that will enable and empower us to not only be honest with those around us, but also honest with ourselves, in a realistic, tangible, and loving way.

THE 6 RULES OF HONESTY

- Memorialize

To *memorialize* is to make it mutual. Honesty must be a two-way street, a shared commitment between both parties. Today, right now, sit down with your spouse and say, "Look, I want to be honest with you from this day forward. I commit to you that I will be honest in everything that I do and my thoughts. And I want you to do the same for me."

Your spouse should say and do the same thing. Now, this doesn't just mean that you're going to be honest with everything. For example, if today I'm at work and I have an indecent thought, I'm not going to call my wife about it. I'm not going to call her and say, "Hey, I just called you because I need you to know that I had this thought about this."

That is not what I mean by honesty. What it does mean is that if my wife were to say to me when I got home today, "What did you do today?" I don't leave anything out, including that indecent thought that I had around lunch time or on that phone call with the client that I really don't like. I don't leave anything out just because I think it may displease her or make me look bad. I don't try to deceive her with my responses, because that would be dishonest.

You may say, "Well, if I don't say anything then I'm not lying."Omission is the same as dishonesty. If you don't share the full truth, you're being dishonest.

Now we are going to touch on this little bit more because there's some gray area here. Sometimes we don't say something just because we're not thinking about it. That's not being dishonest. What I mean here is that when we deliberately and intentionally don't share with our spouse something that they're asking us about or they should know, that's dishonest.

This looks like me going to my wife and saying, "Rhonda, I will

BIFF ADAM

NOT KEEP ANYTHING FROM YOU THAT YOU NEED TO KNOW. I will be honest with you at all times, when you ask me a question. I will answer it the way you want me to." And she will do the same thing for me.

- *Don't Justify*

There is no such thing as little white lies. All small lies or white lies are dishonesty. Perhaps you don't want to say something to your spouse because you know it'll upset them. That's being dishonest. And you might try to justify it in your mind saying, "If I tell her this, she's going to be mad and it's going to ruin all of our plans, so it's better not to tell her." Or, "I'll just share some of the details so it doesn't upset her because she doesn't need to know that I got drunk and drove home intoxicated, so I'll just say I had a few drinks with the guys and came home sometime while she was asleep."

Oh, here's a good one When your spouse asks you how they look in a specific dress or outfit, what are you going to do? I bet every guy just cringed at that, right? Lying has become common place in our culture and we try to justify it with not hurting someone's feelings or thinking they don't need to know it. This is the perceived privacy or protection idea, meaning, this is my personal stuff and they don't need to know about it. It doesn't pertain to them. Or, I'm protecting them by not telling them everything. It would crush them.

Both are seen as okay in our society but both are dishonesty in action and will harm a marriage. If you're willing to be dishonest with the small things, or those things you see as insignificant or *none of their business*, you'll lie with the things that matter.

Smart phones are a big thing for our society today. There is no reason why your spouse should not know the password to your phone and be able to access it at any time. Same thing with bank accounts.

Both spouses should have access and visibility to all accounts and passwords for everything. This includes things with social media, bank accounts, investment accounts, phones, computers, and so forth.

There should always be an open line of communication and honesty between both spouses.

- *Keep It Tight*

Don't confuse honesty with bluntness or rudeness. I touched on this briefly above but I'll go a little deeper for you men here. A great example of where to *keep it tight not blunt* is when your wife might ask you, "Honey, how does this dress make me look? Does it make my hips look too big? Does it make me look fat? Am I still as pretty as I was the day you married me?"

Men, this is a gateway to either glorious bliss or sleeping on the couch. Make your choice wisely, but do so with love and honesty.

Now, this is no problem if you actually think your spouse is the hottest woman to walk the face of the planet (like Rhonda, because she is, not just because I think so) who hasn't aged a second over the last several decades together, and has a body just as toned and on fire as the first time you consummated your marital vows even after birthing two children.

The man who finds a wife finds a treasure, and he receives favor from the Lord[11]. I'm a blessed man!

Let me make it easy on you men. If you always believe and see your wife as a precious jewel from heaven and there could never be anyone as beautiful, smart, riveting, and exciting as she, you'll never struggle to give the right, *and honest*, answer here.

But let's say you haven't quite caught the revelation yet. If she doesn't look good in the dress, the answer shouldn't be, "Yes, you look fat" or "It's the dress, it doesn't flatter you."

You have to be careful and mindful of how you respond. Being blunt is not always the same thing as just being honest. You must be sensitive to her needs. You to her and she to you. Being honest with your spouse is not an excuse to be mean or unloving.

- *Check Your Timing*

Not everything needs to be set immediately. You must pick the correct time for certain things. You know, your spouse is still a human being.

For example, if I need to share something with Rhonda that I know is going to hurt her, and it's something really hard for me to share with her (perhaps something from my past that I've never shared with her before) if she wakes up tomorrow morning with the flu, it's probably not the best time to hammer her with it, right?

You must use common sense when being honest with your spouse. Again, I must emphasize that this does not justify you bending the truth. If she has the flu, then maybe today is not the best time for me to tell her and to wait to pick a better time. Or, if she just found out horrible news that one of her friends or family members has a terminal disease, it's probably not the best time to bring up something I did in the past that will add fuel onto that pain. Make sense?

Now...this does not give you an excuse to put it off indefinitely. You still need to tell her. But maybe what you do is say, "Honey, I know you're not feeling well or you found out some horrible news today, but there's something on your mind that I need to share with you and I'd like to share it with you next week."

Another great way to go about this and picking the right timing to share something with your spouse is to think about it this way. Ask yourself this question:

Is the reason I'm not sharing this with her today for me or for her benefit?

If it's for her; she's feeling sick, she is in grief, and so on, then putting it off is the right thing to do. If it's for you, and you say something around the lines of this, "I want to get lucky tonight, and if I tell her this, sex is off the table" or "I had a great day today and I don't want to ruin that by saying something" then you know what you must do.

If it's for selfish reasons, share it. If it's to protect her and her feelings or her needs, then put it off.

- *Silence Isn't Golden*

We don't just lie with our words, we also can be dishonest by withholding our words. Sometimes we live by holding them and not sharing.

"How did things go today with your boss?" Your wife might ask you.

"It was fine," you say and don't elaborate or tell her that you got laid off and things are not okay financially as a result of being fired and you're stressed out of your mind on how to pay the bills or finding a new job.

This is being dishonest because she could assume that everything *was* okay at work and that you're *still employed.* You might think, "Well, I didn't lie to her." And you might've justified in your mind because you didn't want her to get angry when you told her that you were laid off or to worry her, so you pretended that everything was okay. You know how we men do, right?

I'm the man and I'm supposed to provide for my family and I'll make this work so she doesn't have to worry or be afraid how we'll pay our bills, get groceries, or pay for the kids' college tuition. And, besides, I have an interview next week. I'll have a new job and there will be nothing to worry about. I'll tell her then.

No, no, no! If you're withholding something from you spouse, especially something that impacts her immediately or in the near future, she deserves to know. Your spouse is your teammate; you do life together, not separately. We'll touch more on team in the next chapter.

Whether your spouse will get angry, jealous, insecure, worried, and so forth with something you share, it's important you're honest.

And use common sense to share it at the right time (without waiting too long!).

- *Be Safe Ground*

This is one of the most important ones to remember for both spouses, and plays directly with the last example. Be willing to be transparent and vulnerable with your spouse. Be willing to forgive and offer understanding when your spouse is honest with you. This one is really tough to do.

The first rule is to make a mutual decision to be honest and understanding with one another. That plays a significant role here. If I tell Rhonda that I want her to be honest and that I'm going to be honest with her, I must be careful not to lash out on her when she is honest with me.

It's difficult to be honest with your spouse when you know you're going to get kicked or punched because of what you say. This does not mean that you're supposed to be a door mat to be trampled on. That's not what I'm saying here. What I am saying is that, sometimes when you share something out of pure honesty, maybe you need to take a moment and step away from the situation before responding.

Perhaps you say to your spouse, "Thank you for being honest with me. I need some time to process this before we discuss it further. I need some space so I can gather my thoughts and control my emotions so I don't lash out at you."

A prevalent example of this is unity. Perhaps you have an indiscretion from your past you've never shared with your spouse, so you tell her. It can be anything. Maybe you flirted with another woman, had sex before marriage, did drugs, were addicted to pornography or alcohol, or have a ton of debt.

Whatever it is or was, whether before you met or during your marriage, your spouse needs to know and they understand that by you being honest with them, their responsibility is to preserve that trust and not hold it against you or lash out.

This is a huge deal with marriages we've counseled. We've seen many scenarios where one of the spouses was honest with their husband or wife and then it was used as ammunition against them and held over their head. It's important to accept what your spouse shares, forgive them where needed, and move forward without looking back. If you continuously bring something up to your spouse that they shared with you in trust, they'll resist being honest with you again for fear of retaliation and reprimand.

This is why it's so crucial to be *safe ground* for your spouse, because it will encourage honesty and oneness.

The purpose of pure honesty with your spouse is so they know the real you and develop a close relationship with you. Your spouse should be the only person who truly gets you, dirt and all, and still loves you and stands by your side. That's the power of marriage and honesty when they work together.

If Rhonda shares something with me that she did before we were married and I flip off the handle and say, "I can't believe you did that and didn't tell me! How could you!" and I hold it over her head for years on end, her human instinct of self preservation will kick in, and she'll shut down and never share anything with me again for fear of attack.

It's the same for all of us. No one wants to be shamed, ridiculed, blamed, slammed, or loitered over for the rest of their lives. The best course of action is to thank your spouse for sharing and request some space. And this also pertains to the spouse sharing; you must be willing to give your wife or husband the time and space they need to process what you shared, don't force them to discuss it right then and there on your timetable just because you want to get it off your chest.

Remember the phone test. Does it serve her and protect her, or help you? Your default choice should always be for your spouse's best benefit.

LET THE SCAB HEAL

Sometimes when you're honest with your spouse, you must rip off the scab and let it heal. There's a lot of vulnerability required in marriage with two spouses committed to being honest with one another.

It takes trust, vulnerability, and commitment from both people confessing and sharing with the other. This is a huge sense of unselfishness and selflessness because your spouse may have to say, "What you just told me shattered all trust and hurt me deeply. Thank you for sharing with me, but I need time to digest this. I don't know when I'll be ready to talk, but I'm committed to working through this with you."

If you're the one being honest and sharing, you must give your spouse room to breathe and process when necessary depending on what you share and how they receive it. And if you're the one receiving the revelation or truth, be safe ground for your spouse to share with and honor them by being honest about your feelings and needing time when appropriate. But just as the right timing is critical, don't wait too long to reconvene the conversation if it was something that hurt you.

Get back together, work through it, and keep moving forward as one. This leads into our next point, no secrets in your marriage.

ABSOLUTELY NO SECRETS—EVER!

A secret is a form of dishonesty. There should be no secrets between you. There are five different secrets you should never keep from her spouse if you want to have a forever marriage.

- *Past Secrets*

You should have nothing from your past the your spouse doesn't know about. While your past may not define you as the person you are today, it did play a key role in shaping you into the person you became.

You and your spouse decide to take a cruise ship to the Bahamas to celebrate your fifth anniversary. It's going to be special and the two of you have been wanting to go on a cruise together since you started dating but life kept getting in the way, and then kids came into the picture.

So you had to put off your vacation for several years. You're excited and you look forward to spending one-on-one time with just you and your spouse, no kids, no work, no distractions. Sounds like heaven, right?

There's just one thing. Some old high school friends you haven't told your spouse about suddenly show up at your table during evening meal and surprise you with their presence. You quickly pick up where you left off in your friendship and have a lot of fun.

In this situation, there should never be a thought of, "I hope they don't bring this up in front of my wife." Or in a more direct outcome, your old friends say something that makes you or your spouse uncomfortable and leads to an argument or an intense discussion later on.

There should never be a secret from your childhood or time before you met your spouse that they do not know about. Now, I'm not talking about trivial things like telling your spouse you saw a movie. I'm speaking directly to a conversation that comes up where one of your old friends asks you something like, "Hey, man! You remember Mandy from high school? Man, she's still as wild as she was when she rolled with us. The two of you were the talk of the town. Remember that?"

This is a recipe for disaster for all parties involved and will lead to a rather unpleasant trip to say the least. Your spouse should never have to ask you, "Who is Mandy? What were they talking about?"

The things you shouldn't keep from your spouse, no matter how uncomfortable it may be to tell them about it, consist of things like someone you dated, someone you hooked up with, or got engaged and then broke the engagement off, or you did some illegal thing together. See the difference?

Maybe you had a problem with drugs and alcohol when you were younger or before you met your spouse, they should know about that. You may have kicked the habit a long time ago and not touched a drink or illegal substance in ten or twenty or more years, but that's something they should know even if it's no longer part of your life.

This leads into one of the bigger areas where most people keep secrets or don't disclose the full truth with their spouses for fear of unsetting them, causing a rift in the relationship, or thinking it's not important or relevant since it was before you met them.

- *Sexual Secrets*

This is a big one I've seen in couples we've counseled. And yet, an area that many marriages have failed in. Your struggles with sexual desires or affiliations, whether habitual or dormant, should be shared with your spouse.

It's key to understand that any form of secret forms a stronghold and puts up a barrier between you and your spouse even if you don't realize it.

Sexual sin can be an entire book in and of itself, but I'll keep this simple.

God created you and your spouse as two separate, unique, and individual persons. He made us different than our spouses for a reason. This is what makes marriage so powerful and beautiful.

But, if we keep secrets from our spouse, this beauty becomes darkness and death for a marriage. When God first created Adam in the Garden of Eden, He said it was not good for a man to be alone. And so, God created a help mate for the man.

It wasn't just someone to go and gather fig leaves or cook meals or be your slave and answer to your every beck and call. Spouses are much more than our servant, though God does call us to serve our spouses with unconditional love. This doesn't mean the other person can lord it over them.

Sexual desire is a strong force in most males. Sometimes women have the stronger desire in the relationship, but usually it's the man. For this reason, it's crucial for a man who struggles with lust or sexual sin to confess it and be open about it with their spouse.

How can your spouse help you if they don't know you're struggling with something or did in the past?

Say you watch pornography because you struggle with lust and a need for sexual intimacy. While pornography is not the solution, it's what you were conditioned to accept and the source you went to other than your spouse for sexual needs.

Now that you're married, you have to renew your mind and not watch it anymore (obviously, watching porn is a sin to begin with, but it's even more important you share it with your spouse).

Here's how this might play out.

"Honey, I need to share something with you. I struggle with lust, have my whole life. I used to watch porn every day for release before I met you. I haven't watched it since we've been married, but I slipped and have watched it a few times over the last few weeks. The reason is because I desire sex and need to break this habit. I'm sharing this with you so you can help me overcome this because I want sexual intimacy to only be within our covenant marriage."

This includes all forms of sexual activity, not just physically having an affair with someone else. This involves anything that takes your eyes off of your spouse to fulfill your sexual urges and needs: TV, movies, pornography, magazines, other people, and so forth.

And so, in our example, you may ask your spouse to help you overcome your stronghold. This now goes back to what we mentioned about being safe ground for your spouse. In this situation, the wife has ever right to be angry with her husband, but she shouldn't lash out on him. Instead, she should approach it with understanding and love.

"I understand you looked at porn and why you did, and have in the past. Thank you for trusting me to be vulnerable to share this with me. I need some time to process this before we work through this together. I love you and I'm committed to this marriage. I just need some time."

Your husband may have sinned against you but God can mend and restore all brokenness. You have to give this new revelation your husband shared with you to God and trust Him to see you through it. Here's the harder truth now, you need to help him. And even more powerful than that is the fact that a man is less likely to look at porn after he's had sex with his wife. His desire and need has been fulfilled. That's beautiful...in marriage.

This was the way God intended marriages to function. For each spouse to share their struggles with their spouse to overcome it together and transform into an indestructible force that the enemy cannot defeat.

But what about from a woman's point of view for this same example? She's been wronged, why should he get away with it? Perhaps you might say,

> He wants sex all of the time. I don't feel like having sex. I'm sick.
> I'm tired.
> I'm on my period.
> I'm mad at him for doing this or that or for watching porn. He broke my trust.
> He doesn't help with the kids. He's always working.
> He doesn't help with the chores.

Why should I have sex with him? I don't want to! I'm mad at him and hurt. And maybe you just had an argument and you don't feel that closeness anymore. The truth... none of that matters. You're supposed to meet his needs as he is yours.

Your spouse is your help mate. Maybe you are tired, or you are on your period, or name the situation, there's other ways to help your husband if he needs that sexual release and connection with you.

I'm probably like most men and think sex should be more often than my spouse thinks. And I used to get angry with Rhonda early on in our marriage because I felt like she didn't care about my needs and would make me feel humiliated if she ever said anything other than "yes."

Ever had that in your marriage? It can put a wedge between you, especially if your spouse doesn't know you're feeling this way.

But let me set you men (and woman) free. If your spouse doesn't know, how can they help you? This is where honesty plays an integral part in building your marriage with your spouse. This also goes the other way. If your wife just doesn't want sex as much as you seem to, there are probably reasons for that.

This is where the wife should be honest with her husband. Maybe you're tired because you cleaned the house all day, took care of the kids, took them to daycare and picked them back up, got dinner ready, ran errands, and so forth.

But if all you did was deny your husband sex because you said you were tired and he didn't know why, that could leave him feeling undesired, which in turn, makes you feel unsupported because he's not acting as though he appreciates everything you do, or is still pushing for sex even after you said you were tired. He knew why, right?

Wrong. Our spouses cannot read minds and we shouldn't expect them to. We must tell them how we feel or what we need and keep them in the loop for everything.

Here are a few areas I've heard woman tell us in counseling sessions why they don't want to have sex.

When their husband treats them harshly.
When they don't feel cherished. When they don't feel supported.
When they feel as though they're just an object to their husbands to get off real quick.

They feel disconnected from their husbands.
Their husbands don't help with the chores or kids or meals.
Their kids were difficult and exhausting. They started their period or
are about to.
They feel sick and tired, really.

This is not an exhaustive list but women have also said they feel
more inclined and drawn to have sex with their husbands when they
feel loved, cherished, and their husbands are sacrificial.

Honesty goes both ways. If a woman tells her husband she desires
sex more when he helps with the kids, does chores without her
asking, shows her nonsexual affection, builds her up, the man will be
more inclined to give her those needs as well because he knows
about it.

The key to remember here is to serve your spouse in an unconditional way. What if you were to say, "I really need it right now" but
your spouse just had two kids fighting all day, throw up all over her,
hasn't had a chance to even brush her teeth, and you just had an
argument?

Not exactly an optimal setting for romance, is it? While your
spouse should still meet your need, this is where you should put their
needs above your own.

Maybe you do really need to have sex, but she had a rough day. If
you lay down your life for her as Christ did for the church, you'll put
your own needs aside to build her up. You pursue her righteously to
fully understand her the way she needs to be understood.

Now, if you're just wanting a release and she feels like an object
all of the time, maybe it's time to consider counseling to work through
that with some help. There could be deeper issues going on with both
spouses that the other doesn't know about.

The point is there can't be any secrets. If your spouse doesn't
know what you want or struggle with sexually, this could cause strife
in a marriage. They won't have a clue why you're frustrated, giving
them the silent treatment, or refusing to engage.

Men like a woman to initiate sex. It makes us feel excited and desired. However, many women don't initiate it for various reasons, mainly being they think and desire things differently.

But if a man never tells his wife he would like her to initiate sex from time to time, she'll never know. And if she never tells her husband she's tired, sick, cramping, or that she'd like for him to help out around the house or pursue her throughout the day like he did when they first dated, he'll never know that either.

It's a *give and take* from both parties to grow a strong marriage, one that fulfills each other's needs within the convenient marriage bounds.

Marriage is not like high school where if you got upset with someone you were dating, you gave them the silent treatment and played hard to get. Those childish games are for children, not marriage. And yet, many men and women struggle with this and that's why marriages aren't thriving as much as they could and should.

We counseled a couple once where the man was frustrated that his wife wouldn't initiate sex or that she seemed to never want to have sex and was always complaining about how tired or disinterested she was. Needless to say, this created a rift in their marriage and he began to resent her. And as a result, he treated her with less care and affection and love as she deserved and needed, and it was a negative cycle on itself.

We came to find out that she was okay with initiating sex sometimes, but she didn't know he wanted it. He never vocalized it. So, we came up with a simple solution for them. He would wear his striped socks throughout the day when he was expecting to have sex that evening and this would alert her on his desires.

Each marriage should develop something like this so that there's open and safe and loving communication between spouses, and each person's needs are getting met.

Perhaps you use the sock idea, or come up with a code word like "baking cookies together" or you have sex on the weekends no matter how the week went, or on Mondays, Wednesdays, and Fridays, or every day that ends with "y."

I'm mildly teasing, but you get the jest here. And while I may desire sexual intercourse with my wife more than she does, sometimes I'm not in the mood either and she is. Sometimes I come home from a long day at work or a stressful and intense week and am just *done*. Ever have that feeling? You're just done and want to do nothing but collapse on the bed and let that day or week get erased.

This goes both ways. There have been many times when I'd come home and was hoping or expecting to get lucky that night, but come to find out, she had a rough day. You know, if your spouse or you stays home with the kids while the other goes to work, there are a lot of things that go on during the day.

In our marriage, my career paid a higher salary and so I was the one who went to work while she raised the kids. This was a mutual decision we both came to agreement on. And because she handled the affairs of the house: taking care of the kids, laundry, cleaning, cooking, errands, and so forth, sex was the last thing on her mind after a long day with two little ones.

If you have kids, you know what that's like. If she hadn't been open and honest with me when she had those days, I could have chosen to resent her for not initiating sex or denying me my needs being met.

The key to sexual intimacy with your spouse is open communication and honesty about any past sexual encounters, temptations, sins, strongholds, and current expectations.

And one of the biggest reasons for a lack of intimacy in marriages and one of the top five causes for divorce is finances.

- *Financial Secrets*

Hiding extravagant spending and debt or income bonuses and raises. When we refuse to disclose all knowledge about our finances, whether debt or income, this secrecy creates a mine vs. yours mentality. This leads to eruption in the marriage and a doorway for deceit.

I'm a firm believer in joint accounts for both spouses. Now what I mean by this is that each person has an account for specific purposes, not having private accounts. When you get married, all accounts should be shared and visible and accessible to both spouses.

What is yours is now theirs, both good and the bad. This is how Rhonda and I did it. We each had separate accounts. One account was the debit account and the other was the business account. The debit account was used for all personal experiences for a family. For example, when she would go to the grocery store to get groceries for the week, she would use the debit account.

Each week when I would receive payment from work, I would put a specific amount that we had agreed upon into the debit account. And we both knew that these funds were for her to use to buy groceries, run errands, pay the bills, and so forth.

In the corporate account, or business account, was strictly for business transactions. Each of us had full access and visibility to all accounts. So whenever she would go to the grocery store or pay the bills, there was no secret to what she was spending it on. I could see it.

Finances are a huge deal with marriages. We've seen this be one of the key holdups for spouses that we've counseled. One spouse had an account that the other didn't know about, and used it to pay certain things that were good for the marriage, however their spouse didn't know about it. In this situation, they created the separate account just so they wouldn't bother the other person with having to say something like, "I need this much money to go buy this."

However, we've also seen this abused. For example, one spouse might say they need $300 but in reality, they only need 200. Then they put that extra hundred dollars aside privately. This is a big problem. And it is dishonest. While this might seem like a small thing, it can lead to bigger and more dangerous secrets. And down the road, this path of secrecy could lead to a broken bond of trust between spouses. You do not want to go down that road.

I had a client once years ago with an old company and they were looking into replacing me with another broker. And so their President and Board of Directors were looking to me to see if we could match or beat the deal that this other broker was offering them. Naturally, I asked them to show me what this person was offering them and they agreed.

After reviewing this other broker's proposal, I immediately saw where he was misleading them. He had created a statement under the letterhead and had just copy and pasted another proposal.

So I asked the president if I could meet with the board. He agreed. So when I went to the meeting they were all expecting me to submit my own proposal to either match or beat his. But, all I did when I went in was lay down his proposal and pointed to the discrepancy I had found.

And I said, "Do you see this? Do you see where this looks like this? There's a reason why his looks identical to this other statement. It's because he copied it."

I could feel the tension rise in the room and their eyes shifting to one another.

And I said, "I don't know this guy and I don't want to get into the difference of his proposal my proposal. All I want you to know is my dad told me a long time ago that if someone lies to you about something little, they will lie to you about something bigger."

And I closed my briefcase and walked out. Before I got back to my office, the CEO called me and said, "Don't worry. You're on it."

The point is that any little secret with finances can develop into larger secrets. This is how it is with anything in life, especially with marriages. If you have one small secret about any financial element, it's easier to create another sequence of dishonesty.

And this could be for anything. Take health for example. One spouse might have health related secrets that they aren't sharing with the other spouse. And this could affect any financial decisions. The beauty of marriage is to love and support one another. If there is an issue that one spouse is having that is a health related issue, whether past or present, it needs to be shared with their spouse.

Your spouse is your teammate. They should know everything that's going on in your life. And for practical reasons, they need to know if you're having any kind of health related Issues so they can be praying for you. They need to be able to help and advice you and be able to support you.

If they don't know that you're feeling ill or sick or struggling with something, you could assume that they don't care about you even though they don't know it, or they could go and try to make plans for some kind of vacation, and they don't even realize that you're having financial issues because you're always sick.

And this may be the reason why they're not able to or want to help with the kids, or go to work, or go see their family members, or something like that. But if they didn't tell you, how would you know?

Again, there's a fine line. This doesn't mean every time I have a hang nail I have to tell Rhonda about it. One thing that Rhonda and I do every morning is asked the same two questions to one another.

How did you sleep?
How do you feel?

We try not to make them just like any other two questions and say, "Hey, how's it going?" You know, when someone asks you how you're doing? They don't really want to know the details. They are just saying what's up in passing.

These two questions allow us to know what to expect for the rest of the day. You know, if she were to stay to me, "I slept terrible." Then I know it might be a tougher day. Not only that, I might also then know that I shouldn't make big plans for dinner or go see friends and family or something because she needs to rest. And this might also allow me to know that maybe I should leave work a little earlier that day and get home to cook dinner instead of her having to do it so that she could relax.

It's things like this that we must be aware of when we're living our lives with our spouses. If you have debt, your spouse should know about it. If you got a raise or promotion, your spouse should know about it. If you got laid off and lost your job, your spouse should know about it. If you spent hundreds of dollars on groceries, your spouse should know about it. If you put several thousand dollars into a Roth IRA, your spouse should know about it.

Simple fact is, your spouse should know about every situation with your finances, whether debt or income gains.

- *Relationship Secrets*

Years ago, Rhonda and I were thinking about moving. And so, we started looking at houses. I sort of just browsed, not really taking it seriously. One day she came to me saying, "I found some good houses that I think would be good for us. I'd like to share them with you."

Now, I'm expecting like a two or three bedroom one-story home. You know, a nice and quaint little spread. Instead, when I open up the folder to look at the homes that she had found, they were all 20% bigger than the one we had lived in at that moment.

We both had totally different ideas and visions for what it would look like as empty-nesters when our kids had grownup and had their own families. She wanted a room for every kid and grandkid who had their own homes within five miles of us. And I thought, when would we ever need that many rooms?

And sure enough, now we have our grandkids and children over all of the time. And guess what? Every room is used. We both had totally different ideas of what being an empty nesters would look like. And so this has led to many great conversations to discuss our goals and visions with one another.

One thing I like to do with Rhonda, is when we are driving in the car together, we talk about our dreams and our goals and our vision for families and for each other. It's vital that you are aligned with your spouse in terms of what you want to achieve as a family, in your business, and with your children. You must have a shared vision so that you can both go toward it together.

You need to be aligned with your spouse. You know, you need to discuss what retirement will look like for the both of you. Are you going to move to Hawaii when you retire? Are you going to sell your home and get an RV to travel the country? Are you going to downsize and find the little pad somewhere in the woods near a mountain stream and fish all day?

These are examples of things you'd want to discuss with your spouse ahead of time to ensure you're on the same page with what you want to achieve and do in life. You know, because you're doing life together, not individually anymore.

I've seen so many couples who lacked a shared vision and it caused strife in their marriage or no direction for what they were striving toward together. Discussing something like retirement is not something you want to wait until right before to discuss. Do it when you first get married. Better yet, when you're engaged.

For Rhonda and me, we both had different visions on what being an empty nester looked like for us, and had we not discussed this further (after this initial home search discovery), we could have easily been sidetracked with not sharing the same goals.

I'm not saying that your plans must stay static and unchanging your whole life, just that you have one that you both agree on and are working toward. Plans, goals, and visions change over time and that's okay, so long as you're doing it together.

Vacations are another. Does one spouse want to go on more family vacations than the other? Does your spouse know you want to? Does he or she know what makes you happy about building memories and why vacations is important for you?

If not, start there then map out a vacation to start building those memories you cherish and want to build with your family. And if there's a financial burden that one of you doesn't know about, well, this is a perfect reason why each person knowing everything about the finances and accounts is so that when you do have these discussions for your future, you can plan accordingly, and not get railroaded with the news of, "Hey, we can't go on that dream vacation you planned for our family because I have $50,000 of student loan debt that I never told you about and it's now out of its grace period and interest is accruing."

Don't let this happen to you. Get it all out in the open, work through it together, then start planning your future. This is also why it's so crucial to keep no secrets from your spouse about anything. If you have something sexually you haven't shared with your spouse, now would be a great time. If there's an emotional trauma of some sort from your childhood or upbringing or stronghold you're dealing with and have never healed from (even if you thought you had), share it.

VISION RETREATS

This all plays into setting and creating a beautiful life together as a team and partnership. If you're not emotionally or sexually satisfied or you feel something is lacking in yourself or your marriage, then you may say, "Hey, I really want this" or "I'm not really feeling like this" or "I'm not emotionally there" or "I see a different future and this is why."

Planning for the future and merging your visions for life includes family, friends, each other, children, business, and so forth. Every aspect of life is fair game.

If you've never had this discussion with your spouse, start by sitting down with them tonight after the kids go down (if you have kids) or at dinner (if you don't have kids yet) and ask them, "What does your ideal future look like?"

Then ask the following questions...

What are we doing? Where are we living?

Where are our vacations?
What are we earning? With whom are we spending time?

Jimmy Evans of MarriageToday talks about how he and his wife always go on Vision Retreats every quarter to recalibrate, reconnect, and build their bond.

Vision retreats are when you and your spouse go somewhere just the two of you. No kids. No friends. No family. The sole purpose and goal of a vision retreat is to connect with your spouse and plan your futures together.

You want to plan together. Have fun together. Have a vision together. And this is why vision retreats are so powerful. This doesn't need to be something extravagant where you travel across states or to another country. You can just stay at a local hotel for a day or two, and that'll still be nice.

So what do you talk about in vision retreats? You'll want to ask questions like...

What do you want to achieve individually and as a family?
What do you see as your ideal future? What vacation would you like to do?
What does that look like to you?
How much do you want for retirement?
When do you want to retire? Do you even want to retire? What does that look like?
What are we doing? How much does it cost? Do we want to save for it? Do you even want to save for retirement?
How much do you want in a six-month savings account? Do you want to pay for and save for kids' college education?
How much do we save?

If you don't have kids, you may ask...

Do you want kids?

How many do you want?
How will we raise and discipline them?
What schools will they go to? Will we put them in daycare?

All of these are the kind of questions you discuss at your vision retreat. And each time you go on a vision retreat, these kind of questions and responses may change depending on the season of life you're in.

I recommend that you have these vision retreats at least twice a year, preferably once a quarter. This will allow you to stay calibrated and connected because things shift as the year goes on. You may be one place today and within a few weeks some are completely different.

You establish where you are now and where you want to go. Does this align or does it not? And if there's something that's off or that you both disagree on, now you know what to work on to establish the more ideal plan for you as a couple. Perhaps one of you wants to earn a certain amount of income. Well, your spouse might ask, "Why?"

They may even go as far as to say, "Well, I don't really care about that much." And then you have to decide whether it's reasonable to go after that larger or smaller salary, or if it's a scarcity or poverty mindset or based on some kind of insecurity rooted in something else in your life.

All of these things relate to honesty, open communication, and no secrets. It's not something that you just do once and then you're set for life. This is ongoing and ever evolving. We are creatures that constantly change as life happens and goes on. We adapt, which means our relationship needs to as well.

Honesty should be the foundation for every marriage. There are marriages where it's barely surviving because neither spouse is being completely honest with the other. That is not a forever marriage. Again, they may last forever and be married for a long time, but that is not the definition of a forever marriage.

A forever marriage is one where you are passionately intimate and solely connected with one another, on the same page, the same passions, desires, and working together as a team. You are perpetually improving and growing on a continual basis. If you are just kind of getting by, and treating your spouse like an employee or partner or a colleague or roommate, that is not a forever marriage.

USE COURAGE

You may think that this all sounds good but might be saying, "But there's just one thing I can't share with him or her." If that's the case, then that is exactly what you need to share with them. Now it may hurt or cause temporary division in the marriage, it may take some time to work through it and heal, but everything worth having in life requires courage and sacrifice. Trust me, the juice is worth the squeeze.

If there is a secret, it always comes to the surface eventually. It's better for you to be proactive and share with your spouse on good grounds, and have them help you through it, versus them finding out a different way.

And remember, this requires both sides to be actively engaged with love. This is not a time to tell your spouse all your past mis-steps and expect them to show you grace and forgive you because she has to accept it. Marriage is sacred. It's like your relationship with Christ. When we fully understand grace, then we love Jesus even more and don't want to sin because of that grace. We actually sin less because of it.

And that's how marriage should be with our spouses. When we realize our wife or husband loves us and is showing us grace and forgiveness for certain things, it should make us want to love them and serve them more. We want to do the right thing for them.

So honesty is the main building block to the foundation of a forever marriage. And also probably one of the hardest ones for most people to be vulnerable and transparent about.

HONESTY RECAP

- The *6 Rules of Honesty*: don't memorialize, don't justify, keep it tight, check your timing, silent isn't golden, and be safe ground.
- NO secrets in your marriage: past, sexual, financial, relational.
- Vision Retreats are necessary to establish a shared vision and goal for your marriage.

LOVE IN ACTION

- Which of the *6 Rules* do you struggle with? Which does your spouse struggle with?
- How can you enhance and improve those?
- What secrets of your past, sexual, financial, or relationships have you not shard with your spouse?
- Sit down with your spouse and share any secrets still in the dark.

---

1. 1. http://www.in2013dollars.com/us/inflation/1940?amount=1000
2. 1. http://www.in2013dollars.com/us/inflation/1940?amount=40000
3. James 1:27
4. Romans 2:12-16
5. Proverbs 14:12
6. Ephesians 4:25
7. Zachariah 8:16
8. Proverbs 12:22
9. Hebrews 4:13
10. Proverbs 23:7a NKJV
11. Proverbs 18:22 NLT

3

TEAM

I have a client, who is also now a friend, who's sixty-five years old at the writing of this. Many people don't like him because he comes off as harsh and brash. His wife is the same way and I'm not sure how they've survived this long in their marriage. It's each of their second marriage but it's going for over twenty years now.

In truth, their marriage is succeeding because they realized they're both on the same team and not enemies. Years ago, he came to me stressed out with his marriage. He asked how Rhonda and I made it look so simple.

After clarifying no marriage is easy, I shared with him a simple principle that has enabled us to thrive for so long. It's the principle of team.

I told him, "You and your wife are on the same team. Your two girls (who were still teenagers at the time) are not on your team."

He looked at me shocked and a bit confused.

"Let me explain," I said. "When you and your wife got married, who did you marry?"

He said his wife's name.

"Did you marry your parents?" I asked. He shook his head.

"Did you marry your friends, coworkers, or children?"

Again, he shook his head. He was beginning to see the picture. "When you got married, you may have had friends and family there to support you, but they weren't sealing a covenant bond with you that they committed to upholding and cherishing for the rest of their lives. Each of them, while they may love you, will never love you the way your wife will be able to nor have the same intimate connection and relationship as you can with her."

It's more easily acceptable for the man to grasp how friends and family aren't on the team, but for women, it's harder to accept that their children aren't on their team. But, children are a temporary assignment from God. They're given to us to train and build up in God's truth so they can go on to be disciples of Christ with their own families and in the world.

"You must realize that the circle is only the two of you. Sometimes others intertwine their circles with you for a period of time, but it's never the heart of your relationship. That must remain only with the two of you."

This is where most marital problems come up because one of the spouses (or both) has allowed something or someone else to enter into their sacred circle that doesn't belong. It's like allowing acid to leak into your water. You may not taste it the first few drinks from the faucet, but after awhile, that acidity will wreak havoc on your body.

Now, I'm not saying that all things and relationships are acidic, just that they could become so in your marriage if you're not careful and keep them in their place of priority.

We talked about the idea of team for several hours until it clicked in his mind. I wasn't sure how he would receive advice from me because he's older and he never takes advice well from anyone.

Since that day, he has told me on numerous occasions how that one conversation and the principle of team changed his marriage. It's worth noting that they both attend church, they don't curse at each other and there's no issue of infidelity. But he's said that they use that principle to remind each other when they're at each other's throats (usually over petty things like we all do) that they have each other's back.

For him, he keeps things from her pertaining to his business, and those *secrets* cause a rift between them until he remembers she's on his team and needs to know. However, the problem with her is she always second guesses him and never listens to what he has to say.

When he brings something up, she'll instantly play devil's advocate and shut down everything he said. She's automatically thinking it's wrong just because he said it. I had to coach him on this.

I told him, "Next time she does this, ask her what she'd say if her best friend had the same thought. Would she respond the same way? Would she automatically think negatively about it? And after she had a chance to respond, remind her that you're on the same team."

Your spouse is your teammate. It's you two against the world. It's easy to get into fighting mode or defensive and forget that your spouse has your best interests in mind, sometimes they just need reminding that you're for them, not against them.

EVERY MEMBER COUNTS

In American football, you have eleven men on the field who work together for a specific goal, whether defense or offense. When you're out on the field, you're lined up in formation to either try to score on the other team or shut their offense down.

In order to do this, every member of the team must execute their role perfectly or it won't work. Take the center and quarterback for example.

Let's say the quarterback hates the center. He just can't stand him, doesn't like him as a person, and he always gets on his nerves. They never hang out during school or after practice. And he makes and effort to avoid any contact with him more than he absolutely needs.

However, when game day comes, they both put those differences aside. If not, they won't win. If the quarterback doesn't trust his center or treats him negatively or if they don't remember they're on the same team, he won't block, and as a result, the quarterback will get sacked every time.

While you may hate each other off of the field, during game time, you're partners and work together. The principle of team is a mentality that every couple must understand and put into action.

Out of the five key pillars for a successful and forever marriage, team is one of the hardest because it's a paradigm shift that must form.

MARRIAGE IS A CHOICE

Rhonda and I were recently at a wedding and the DJ had all married couples come to dance floor. He had us stand in rows and asked, "If you've been married five years or less, sit down."

Several couples walked back to their seats.

"If you've been married for ten years or less, sit down."

More went to their seats. He continued doing this until Rhonda and I were the last ones standing. For the first time in our lives, we were the longest married couple in the room. I guess that means we're old. Well, I am, Rhonda never ages.

Everyone cheered for us and I got to walk my lovely bride back to her seat of honor. It was nice. But, I say all of this to paint a clear picture that, while being married for over thirty-five years is awesome, it doesn't necessarily mean you have a forever marriage.

A forever marriage is more than a long marriage. I'm sure you've seen couples who have been married for many decades and they couldn't be more miserable and disconnected than a toad in a boiling pot.

Those couples are just married, or living partners at that point. There's no love, no fire, no passion, no intimacy. They're essentially roommates. While they don't believe in or think they should get divorced, which is good, what kind of marriage is that?

It shouldn't be, "I'm married because I don't want to get

divorced." It should be, "I'm married because I can't imagine another day or second without my spouse by my side."

And before you start to think Rhonda and I some prodigy or unicorns, we aren't. We still fight. We still disagree. We still must constantly remind ourselves and one another that we're on the same team and we aren't going anywhere no matter what.

A forever marriage doesn't mean you never fight, or argue, or have disagreements. Through all of the ups and downs you'll experience in your marriage, I want for you to enjoy the intertwining and beauty of each other. The happiest day of my life should be with my spouse, not fishing, hunting, playing golf, shopping, traveling, and any number of things you love doing.

RATE OF DIVORCE

If you've ever stopped to see what the rate of divorce is in America, it's pretty interesting. One thing that shocked me (and also didn't) was the fact that Nevada has a 28.6% divorce rate. So, based on every 1,000 people, roughly 28 of them get divorced.

Why would there be such a high rate of divorce in Nevada? Any guesses? What is in Nevada that people love going to for gambling, events, parties, worldly endeavors, and like?

Las Vegas, you got it! One reason for the influx of divorces in Nevada is because of the many chapels there and the fact that many people get married on a whim. And the next day, or a few weeks later, they realize what they've done and this person they met at the bar, the club, or the gambling table isn't the person they remember.

On the opposite end of the spectrum is Delaware. It has the lowest divorce rate, as well as Illinois at 9.5%. But you might be saying, "Wait a minute! I thought the divorce rate was around 50%?" It is and it isn't.

I'll explain.

These are the annual rate of people that get married who also then got divorced in that state that year. While the national divorce rate has hung around 50% for the last forty years. Let's look at some more stats.

By the age of 30, 75% of women have been married, and 50% have cohabitated outside of marriage. This is not good when we look at the probability of the first marriage ending in divorce within the first five years of marriage. It's 20%.

And what do you think happens to those who cohabitated before marriage? It's even higher. And then you get the scenario of infidelity. Marriages that come out of an affair that lead to divorce skyrocket. Why?

Because when you cheat on your spouse with someone you claim is your soulmate and your true love, the simple fact is, if you cheat once, you're more likely to cheat again. After years of marriage, the probability of divorce is 1 in 3 staying married, and that doubles if you lived together before marriage.

My goal is for everyone reading this to have the kind of marriage that in ten years, you're more passionately in love and working together than when you first got married. In the last chapter we discussed honesty and how to be honest in all things. This chapter we're going to discuss team. In order to have a forever marriage you must have honesty, team, contentment, spirituality, and unselfishness. We'll get into the next three in the coming chapters.

If you do all of these, your marriage will be a forever marriage, and in ten years, you'll be thriving not surviving. It'll no longer be, "We need to try not to divorce because God hates divorce." If we keep these five reminders in our minds and marriages, the longevity of a marriage will take care of itself.

DIVORCE RATE DECREASING

Do you know what the current national divorce rate is in America? If you guessed 49%, then you're right. Why do you think the rate is going down? One factor is people are choosing not to get married. Another is they wait to get married when they're older.

Do you think couples are more or less likely to get divorced if they married before the age of 25? While they are less likely, the surprising thing is it's not by much more. It's only a few percentage points lower than the national average. There are several factors that play a role in that, but let's dive into how you can elevate your marriage to have a 100% success.

WHO MAKES UP YOUR TEAM

Your team is you and your spouse. Period. It's not your parents, their parents, your friends, their friends, colleagues, or your children. It's only the two of you.

Genesis 2:24 makes it very clear that, "a man shall leave his father and his mother and hold fast (cleave) to his wife and they shall become one flesh (person/entity)."

Now before you ladies say, "It only told the man to leave and cleave," it's talking to both genders. This doesn't mean we ignore our parents and kick them out of our lives because the Bible also tells us to honor and respect our parents, and as a result, things will go well for you and you live a long life[1].

You should continue a relationship with your parents, but here's the thing. Your parents should know, and if they don't, you need to make this clear, that if you have to choose between them or your spouse, you will choose your spouse every time.

I have a wonderful relationship with my parents. My dad was my best man in our wedding. He'll be 88 this year. He loves to give hugs to the pretty girls. When you're old, you can get away with a lot of things.

They are close to Rhonda and me. Early on in our marriage, they felt like they needed to tell me how to live my life and my marriage. Now, don't misunderstand me. They meant well, and they love us dearly, they just were poking their nose where it shouldn't have been. Eventually, this created a spark (to say it lightly), because they were getting too personal. As a matter of fact, one of the first things they said to Rhonda and I after we got married was, "Y'all better not get divorced because if you do, we get Rhonda." Ouch!

They love her dearly. However, it got to a point where I had to say, "Don't make me choose between you and Rhonda, because you'll lose."

I'm 56 and we've been married over 35 years, with two children who also have children of their own, and our relationships with them and our parents are stronger than ever. I was 25 when I said those words. It wasn't easy by any means, but it was necessary. If you're hesitant to make that stand because you think it'll shatter your relationship with your parents, it won't. It's just you and your spouse stating that you're a team and you will back each other up.

This statement kickstarted our marriage how it should be. This is a huge deal among millennials today, especially since there is usually one parent or set of parents who tries to control the marriage.

It's great if your parents are involved in your life. Ours go on vacations with us, but there needs to be a line drawn in the sand when it comes between you and your spouse. All this does is create a hierarchy that makes it easier to have boundaries. If you have a parent like this, I'm sure your spouse is nudging you right now.

US AGAINST THEM

A marriage is you against the world. I don't mean this negatively as you should engage with those around you and establish strong relationships outside of your marriage, but it's a rule to live by when the rubber meets the road.

Ecclesiastes 4:9 says that, "Two are better than one because they have a good reward for their toil." While this can involve friends and other believers, it's also speaking to marriages.

Two married people, sticking together, are stronger than one. Don't do things alone. Even God said it was not good for man to be alone in the Garden[2].

It's crucial to realize that, and this will be really hard for some of you (especially women), your kids are not on your team. I'm sure some of you grunted right there. It's hard to accept this truth. Trust me, I know.

It's even harder for mothers because of their maternal instinct and bond with their children. You should love your children as I'm sure you do if you have kids. You should take a bullet for them if the situation called for it (hopefully it never does). You should have that kind love for your children.

The only thing is you have to realize is that God gave them to you as a temporary assignment. You raise them, care for them, protect them, instruct them, train them, and then let them go.

THE DEVIL WANTS TO DESTROY YOUR MARRIAGE

The world would like nothing more than to see your marriage fail. And the devil will use anything you allow him to in order to destroy your bond and relationship with your spouse. He'll even use good things like church, friends, children, work, parents, and siblings to break you apart. You know, important things.

There is nothing wrong with any of those when they're in their proper place and priority. As a matter of fact, those are great things. You should cherish your kids, your friends, and your family, but they aren't your team.

In February 1919, President Woodrow Wilson had a nervous breakdown and a cerebral hemorrhage, which left him paralyzed. His wife, Edith, was with him when he had a terrible seizure. Now, back then the Internet didn't exist and so things could be kept hush-hush unlike today.

Around the same time as this he had an important Treaty that he was pushing for with Congress. And even though he had had the seizure, he was still President. It was crucial this Treaty passed. It was months before Congress or anyone outside of the inner circle knew about his condition because his wife stepped in and communicated for him.

While physically he was incapable of his previous duties, he was still mentally all there. And so, she would tell people he was under the weather.

That's how powerful your marriage can be when you work as a team. Nowadays with the Internet and social media and the news outlets, if something happens, we all know about it. Back then though, even the highest office in the country was guarded, shielded, and protected by a spouse.

YOUR SPOUSE IS NOT YOUR ENEMY

Have you seen the movie Mr. & Mrs. Smith? I love the movie poster. It has Brad Pitt and Angelina Jolie standing back to back with their suppressed (silencer) guns raised. Neither of them knew the other was an assassin, working for opposite intelligence organizations, ordered to kill the other.

Even Hollywood got it right this time. Marriage is a spouse and a spouse against everyone else, no matter what they're ordered to do. The gun that you have in your hands is not for them, it's for tearing down strongholds and every high place that exalts itself above the Lord[3].

Isn't it ironic how we often treat our spouses as our worst enemies? We tend to treat them worse than we would a stranger. Why is that?

Have you ever gone to church together and fought on the way? You spoke real nasty to one another, but once you walk through the doors, you act like nothing happened.

You see someone you know or from your life group or the greeter and say, "Hey! Good to see you."

They ask, "How are you?"

Your spouse says, "We're doing great. Thank you."

And you're thinking to yourself, "If you had been in the car just a few minutes ago, you'd know we are not fine. Don't let her smile fool you. The words that came out of her mouth could cut butterfly wings."

Or perhaps you'd think, "I wish she would act that way and talk to me like that. She treats everyone else with more respect and honor and kindness than me."

It shouldn't be this way.

KIDS WILL CHALLENGE YOUR TEAM

If you have kids, perhaps you've experienced this next example. One day our son asked Rhonda if he could have something. I don't remember what it was, other than that it was before dinner and she told him to wait until after we ate. Well, like a kid does, he then came to me and asked, "Dad, can I have this?"

Being the smart husband that I am (this time), I asked him, "What did your mother say?"

I watched as his demeanor changed from joyful, happy, and smiling to sour and frowning.

"No fair," he said.

"Whatever your mother says, I support. She and I are a team."

Men, here's a pro tip for you. This is extra and free. If you want your spouse to look at you with eyes of admiration and respect, and potentially, add those valuable brownie points to get to the "might get lucky" level, always back your wife.

With all kidding aside, it's vital for your kids to see you on the same page, working together, not against one another, and not slamming the other.

Have you ever seen this situation go a different way? Maybe you're at the store or a restaurant and you hear a kid ask for candy at the checkout aisle.

"Daddy, can I have this?"

"You know I would, but your mom said no." "So, can I have it?"

Husband doesn't even blink because his wife isn't there. "Sure, just don't tell your mom. This can be our little secret."

Do not do this. If you have, don't beat yourself up about it, and if you have a spouse who has (or still does) done this, don't point the figure and criticize them either. Just learn from this and do better next time.

Our kids need to see we support our spouse's decisions, even if it goes against what we'd like to do or how we'd raise them. Maybe you're the spouse who would let your kids have that candy before dinner but your spouse says they must eat their dinner first before they can have candy, or watch TV, or whatever it is.

Regardless of your preference, if your spouse said something, you should honor that. If you disagree, then wait until you're together privately to discuss and share how you'd rather do something different.

See how we're involving honesty and team at the same time? This is how marriages get stronger and each person increases the other into a better person. Neither of us is perfect, we never will be. But, by working together, what might be a weakness for one can be improved by the strength of the other.

The key is we're presenting a solid and consistent front to our kids, friends, family, and others. It also teaches our kids that they can't always get their way and must learn to respect authority, others, and later, their spouses.

Kids are the best at innocent manipulation and pulling your strings. They don't need to learn this, it's innate in each of them. And if you have toddlers, you know this all too well. As they grow into teenagers, it just shifts into a different form of resistance.

Don't worry. You'll overcome those trials and exciting times together. And maybe you were raised where if one parent said something, you'd go to the other because you knew they'd say, "Yes." If you and your spouse are at odds with one another, you should still support them and not go against their wishes just to spite them. This is easier said than done, but you can do it. I believe in you.

If you want your children to grow up and have their own healthy marriages, you must show them what a healthy marriages looks like.

5 FACTORS TO A SUCCESSFUL TEAM

Let's look at the five key factors to team in our marriages. These will act as a guidepost whenever a grey area arises, and they will, or you're faced with resistance, whether internal or external.

- *Commitment*

A couple must be committed to their marriage. They must be committed to honesty, faithfulness, and lifelong love (and the pursuit thereof).

If you were married recently or within the last few years, your vows may still be fresh on your mind. But if you were married many years ago, your vows should still be on top of your mind. Just because you may have said, "Until death do us part" or "in sickness and in health" doesn't mean that you don't wake up every day with the same fervor, commitment, and passion toward your spouse, their well-being, and your marriage.

Each and every day you have to renew your love for your spouse. You can't live off of the high of yesterday or the honeymoon phase. You can't depend on the fact that you were kind to your spouse yesterday, got her flowers, gave her diamond earrings, or that you helped with the kids and chores.

Just like the Israelites, we must gather our manna each and every day. If we try to hoard it or store it up, it'll spoil. If we are attentive and intentional with our spouses every day, we are prone by nature, to become stagnant and disengaged. It's easy to do so when you're stressed, running on fumes because the kids won't sleep, or work is demanding.

You must renew it daily. One of the pillars we'll discuss in the last chapter is selfishness. It's in our fallen DNA to make up every morning and think about ourselves.

"I've got to take care of myself. I need to fulfill and satisfy my needs. If you get in the way of me, I'll crush you or leave you behind."

It's our nature to act and think this way, even if we don't realize we are doing so. The Bible teaches repeats over and over again that we must say no to self, pick up our cross, and follow Christ. Just as Jesus submitted to the cross to save us because He loved and cherished us so much, we must do the same for our spouse.

- *Communication*

We touched on this some in the chapter on honesty, but let's go a little deeper. Communication and honesty go hand-in-hand. We must constantly communicate our thoughts, ideas, plans, hopes, dreams, goals, fears, doubts, and opinions with our spouses. We must share our feelings.

When communication between spouses goes silent, it's usually a bad sign. When this happens, your marriage grows cold, distant, unsatisfying, and abrasive. Everyone suffers.

We also must communicate so we don't clam up and shut down. The devil is out to steal, kill, and destroy, and seeks whom he may devour. He knows that if he gets us alone, he can destroy us. This is why solitude is never the solution. If you're unable to speak with your spouse, seek counsel so a third party can aid the communication.

This plays into the notion that if your spouse does open up, and they share their feelings or thoughts or opinions, and you don't like it, you don't jump down their throat and lord it over them, and punish them for the rest of your life.

You don't want to say something like, "You're too sensitive."

That will destroy a person's confidence, especially men, and they will never open up to you again. We want to be sure we're safe ground for our spouses so they keep an open line of communication with us, and the same goes for your spouse.

If you notice your spouse is more quiet lately, ask them, "Honey, you've been quiet lately. Is something on your mind?"

Keep in mind, this shows them that you are safe ground and they can open up to you. It's not always something vital or life-changing. It could just be they have things on their mind about work, their bodies, their passions, and so forth. Don't immediately assume your spouse is holding something from you if they go silent.

I will say though, if your thoughts are drifting or meditating on something to the point it's stressing you out or causing you anxiety and fear, your spouse needs to know about that right away.

Sometimes it's something shallow and easily remedied, or, other times, it'll mean you have to live with it, swallow it, and step back to let it set in before responding.

No matter how seasoned you may think your marriage is or how long you've been together, whether you're brand new or going on fifty years, you must communicate.

COMMUNICATION IS 93% NONVERBAL, 7% VERBAL

We are communicating whether we think we are or not. You may think you're not speaking to your spouse but you are. If no words are coming out of your mouth, then a slew of them are emitting from your body language.

Studies have shown that 93% of our communication is nonverbal and stems from our tone, behavior, attitude, and demeanor.

If your spouse has ever said, "I don't like how you speak to me. You always have a harsh tone" or "I know what you meant, because your eyes told me." There's reason for this. Our minds are conditioned to notice and take in all senses. Without us consciously taking action, our eyes, ears, nose, and bodies gather information about our surroundings and environment and situations nonstop.

This is why sometimes you could be somewhere and suddenly feel uneasy. While there's a spiritual side to this, it's also because your mind has saved every memory, and it immediately (in a split second) equates whether you've encountered something similar and whether you should flee.

I've also seen the converse in effect. Has anyone ever told you that you look angry all of the time? And you say, "I'm just thinking. This is my normal face."

This is also true. Sometimes there is really nothing going on and we misinterpret our spouse's facial expressions or body language for ill, and it could just be that they have gas or a headache.

The key: show grace and talk.

- *Coordination*

When our kids were younger, I used to raise my voice when I was frustrated and Rhonda would be standing behind them mouthing to me, "Lower your voice. Watch your tone."

She's better at that than me and she helped me improve in that area with our children and with her by supporting me and reminding me of my tone, body language, and attitude. It affects everyone, especially little children because they're a sponge and suck everything up, good and bad.

YOUR SPOUSE'S STRENGTHS COVER YOUR WEAKNESS

Use each other's gifts, talents, and strengths to improve your marriage, service others, and love on each other. Life is smoother when we're coordinating as a team and utilizing all of the resources we have available to us.

Remember, God placed you and your spouse together for a reason. You complete one another. What you need, they have. And what they need, you have.

This is a common stereotype among women. If your wife is analytical and great with T-charts, she probably should be handling the checkbook and bills. If you have no idea how to balance a checkbook, pay bills, set up auto payments, handle investments, and they do, you know who should focus on it.

You were put together for a reason. Use each other's talents and abilities. And it is true, opposites do attract. When you notice your spouse is better at something than you are (even if it goes against the stereotypical and societal norm), let them excel there and build them up. Coordinate together to maximize your strengths and cover your weaknesses.

If your husband is amazing at cooking and folding laundry, let him. If your wife earns more at work and it makes more sense for her to keep working and you stay home with the kids, do it.

Remember, you're a team and everything you do either makes your team stronger or weaker.

HANDLE EACH OTHER WITH UNDERSTANDING

"Likewise, husbands, live with your wives in an understanding way, showing honor to the woman as the weaker vessel, since they are heirs with you of the grace of life so that your prayer may not be hindered.[4]"

The point he's making here is to know your spouse and be considerate. When both people are considerate, communication and coordination improve. Be considerate. Be sweet. Be kind.

- *Clarity*

Without clarity of vision, there is no goal or direction. I like the saying, "If you aim at nothing, you'll probably hit it."

Dream big and dream together. Walk in the same direction. If you're reading this and you don't know what your spouse's dreams are then that's your mission today. Wait for the opportune time to speak, when the kids go off for a nap or on the way home.

Go up to them and ask, "What are your dreams? What do you want out of life?"

They may shrug and say they don't know or give you a blanket statement of, "For u s to love each other and make memories with our kids." If they give you a Hallmark answer, you know, "That we're happy and go on vacations together to make memories" then probe them to go deeper. If they struggle to give you specifics, then you may have uncovered a stronghold in their lives that's preventing them from dreaming bigger. If you're the dreamer in your marriage, this is where you leverage your strength to bring your spouse up to your level.

If they aren't where you are, don't chastise them or belittle them. Give them time to get to where you are, and likewise, for them with you.

Start with specifics.

"Where do you want to be in five years? Do you want to still be living where we are? Do you want a bigger, smaller, or newer house? Do you want to go on two vacations together as a family and one together? If so, where?"

Ask about the kids, homes, vacations, retirement, money, investments, each other, sex, charity, and so forth. And if your spouse still has a hard time coming up with deeper ideas, share yours with them and tell them why you have those and where they fall in with that.

If you add commitment, communication, and coordination together, you get contentment.

- *Contentment*

Contentment doesn't mean you don't want more out of life, it just means you're satisfied with where you are because you're working as a team. We'll dive deeper into this in the next chapter as it's one of the pillars to a forever marriage.

NON-TEAM THOUGHTS

I want to close this chapter with one last thought. Non-team thoughts. These are those thoughts where you might say, "I can't believe she said that. Why doesn't she treat me as well as she does a stranger? I should just go watch porn because I'm tired of hearing how tired and disinterested in sex she is" and so on.

When these thoughts come, and they will, just remember the person you're unhappy with at that time still has your back. Your spouse wants the best for you. Many times, especially in the heat of the moment or when we're hurt or discouraged, or disappointed, we lose that realization. In fact, that may be the root of the problem in the first place.

Your spouse loves you more than anyone else. Your spouse is your soulmate. Rhonda and I have been married for over thirty-five years now. We actually dated for six years before we got married, so we've been together for over forty-one years. That's a long time to be with someone.

And let me tell you, it's still as exhilarating now as it was when we first kissed. The first date we had my dad had to drop us off at the theater because we were both too young to drive. We've been together since.

I guess you could say that movie sealed the deal. We dated for several years before marrying, but let me tell you a little secret (don't worry, Rhonda knows this!), there probably couldn't be any more different two people on the face of the planet. And honestly, we still aren't alike. And you know what's really amazing? How much we are alike in our differences.

Even though we've been together for forty-one years and married for thirty-five, we've had to grow together and still are. We're no fairy-tale marriage no matter how awesome we look on the outside.

Marriage is work, and when you work together, you create something remarkable.

Perhaps you're reading this and thinking, "You and Rhonda are perfect. You don't know my spouse or my situation. It'll never work out."

The simple truth...there were times early on (and still) where I was going "Argh!" and she was going "Argh!" with each other. That's marriage for you, but we never abandoned the commitment to pursue one another and do it as a team.

We're committed to making our marriage a forever marriage; a marriage we want every day. And so, we work on it and never give up. I want the same for you.

TEAM RECAP

- Your marriage has a 100% chance to succeed and thrive.
- Your team is only comprised of you and your spouse. Your children, friends, parents, coworkers are not on your team.
- Your team mentality is the power source to crush life together.
- To be a team, you need commitment, communication, coronation, clarity, and contentment to create a forever marriage.

LOVE IN ACTION

- Write down who is on your team.
- Write down the areas you feel your spouse isn't on your team or goes against you.
- Write down what you consider the solution to those.
- Discuss these with your spouse and make a commitment to be on each other's team no matter what.
- Confront anything and anyone who is pulling you or your spouse from your team and set those boundaries.

---

1. Exodus 20:12
2. Genesis 2:18
3. 2 Corinthians 10:3-5
4. 1 Peter 3:7

4

CONTENTMENT

Are you content in your marriage? In your life? In your work or career? In your relationships with your friends and family? In your sex life, finances, health, and desires?

Many people confuse contentment with not wanting more. They feel that if they desire more or to attain more that they're greedy or discontent. This couldn't be further from the truth. Another way to say contentment is satisfied, happy, joyful, fulfilled.

DISCONTENTMENT

What does it look like to be discontented? Contentment is a bit more abstract and easy to misunderstand or lead to living an unfulfilled life for fear of the perception of discontentment. While discontentment can lead to ungodly activities, such as idolatry, which leads to selfishness, it's deeper than that.

Contentment is not having the things you want, but wanting the things you have.

It's being satisfied with where you are and what you have right now. Meaning, you don't need more to feel happy or satisfied. If you got more, great, but you don't need it to feel complete or happy.

Contentment is ideological, much like fairy tales. Many women believe that their husbands should resemble Prince Charming from story books, movies, and Hallmark shows. He's supposed to be this knight in shining armor, strong, handsome, rich, and conquers the world with a word.

He's...

Always a gentleman. Always kind.
Always generous. Always selfless. Always a servant.
Always a great provider. Always the best protector.
Always...[fill in your greatest desire].

Isn't that right? Now, you may not consciously think this, but it's imbedded into each of us through media. This is equally true for men.

This is also why pornography and graphic movies are so enticing to many men (and women) and causes them to struggle with lust, because our culture says that you'll marry a porn star that will fulfill every sexual fantasy and desire at your beck and call with the snap of your fingers.

She'll...

Always want to have sex. Always initiate it.
Always enjoy it.
Always do whatever position you want. Always do it as often as you want.
Always be toned, fit, and wear sexy outfits. Always be adventurous.
Always...[fill in your greatest desire or wish].

Isn't that right, men? And society tells us that if these things aren't happening and we aren't fulfilled sexually with our wives, that we married the wrong woman and we should go out and find our fun somewhere else.

What's even more sad is that this doesn't stop at just our romantic or sexual assumptions and expectations, it overflows into every aspect of our lives.

She must cook this way.
Our house must be this big and in this location. Her SUV
must always be clean.
He must always be clean shaven, ripped, and earn multiple
six-figures every year.
We must go on this many vacations.
Our children should act like this or go to this school and get
this job.

And when they or something in our lives doesn't fit this mold, we become discontent and unhappy because we've believed a lie. A forever marriage means you're still passionately in love with your spouse even when they're in the bathroom throwing up, have the flu, pooping their brains out because they ate your undercooked dinner the night before, tired and stressed from the kids and doesn't act engaged during sex, or just wants to sit at home and never leave.

A forever marriage is being content no matter the situation. You love them unconditionally; flaws, poop, throw up, and all. Anything else is selfishness and leads to dishonesty, which leads to a lack of team mentality, which leads to worse things.

I love the U2 song, "I Still Haven't Found What I'm Looking For." When Bono wrote that song, no one knew he was a believer. And isn't it ironic how spot on that song is about our lives and our relationships? It's kind of how we go through life, isn't it?

I'm still out there searching...

WANTING MORE IS NOT DISCONTENTMENT

Many people nowadays take this to the extreme and go, "I agree with you, Biff. We need to be content." And then they stop pursuing any growth. Some people are Type A personalities and they build huge networks and businesses, and yet, we might be tempted to say they aren't content.

Why is that? Is it wrong to want more? Is it a bad thing to pursue growth in our resources and life?

There's a large misconception that says you can't have drive, you can't be passionate, you can't want more, you can't go after more because then you're not content. It's key to remember there's a difference between content and love. It's more, "I'm grateful and satisfied and enjoying what I already have, and at the same time, going after more to be better, to grow, to leave a bigger impact on the world."

It's okay to want more and to achieve more. God is a god of increase, not the status quo. He expects us to increase and grow what He's given us. The reason...to bless others and glorify Him.

On the converse, there's also a misconception that if you're content, you're lazy. This then means that discontentment is associated with drive and passion. This couldn't be further from the truth as well.

The key is to look at the end game. What is the purpose of wanting or not wanting more? Is your purpose to generate a million dollars every single year to make you feel good, boost your confidence, and feed your ego, or is it to use those resources to bless and serve others, while also enjoying the fruit of your labor?

Just like with each of our five pillars for a forever marriage, the trick is to always look at it from the end goal and outcome. If it's to serve your spouse or others, it's selfless. If it's to serve you and your own ego and pride, it's selfish. If you can be happy with never getting more money, more fame, more recognition, more sex, more whatever...then you're content. If you constantly need more of anything to feel fulfilled, then you may want to examine your motives.

COMPARISON IS A DEATH TRAP

God wants us to be content. We see this all throughout the Bible. We see this in Paul's life. Where Paul was unbelievably wealthy, even as a very, very young man, a part of the Sanhedrin, and he gave it all up and became basically a pauper missionary for the sake of Christ.

No, you do not need to be poor to be a good Christian and spouse. So long as your possessions don't possess you, you're good.

In America, contentment is a lost form. If you were to drive home today from work, you will see advertisements and billboards designed to make you feel less satisfied with your life and like you're missing something, that you won't be complete or happy unless you have this new car, this bigger home, these friends, this income, this hot wife.

It's all over the billboards on the highways. It's on the radio in your car. When you get home, it's on the TV and movies. We're constantly bombarded by "your life isn't good enough unless you have this..." Fill in the blank.

And because of this constant barrage of greed and discontentment, coupled with our fallen nature, it's tough to be content in our marriages. You know, we see the best in other people's marriages, and the worst in ours, and we start to wish our spouse was like theirs.

Ladies, you may see posts and pictures on Facebook or Instagram of a friend or other women whose husbands took them on these extravagant vacations, dining at exquisite restaurants with immaculate service, massages, pedicures & manicures, food delivery, and walking on the beach hand-in-hand or sailing off into the horizon on a private yacht.

And you might be tempted to think, "I wish my husband would do that for me, take me on those trips, earn that much money, speak to me that way. She's so lucky!"

Or husbands, you may see other entrepreneurs, influencers, or successful business owners who are super wealthy, fly personal jets and helicopters, never deal with traffic because they have someone who drives them and a private security detail to get them through the long lines, or a super hot wife that's always dressed like she's a Victoria's Secret model and constantly showering her man with kisses, affection, kind and encouraging words, and chasing him for sex. And you might be tempted to think, "I wish my wife looked like that and treated me that way. He's so lucky!"

And before you know it, discontentment has rooted in your heart and you begin to loathe and resent your spouse or your life and envy other's. God did not create marriage or life to function this way.

ENVY BREEDS ANXIETY

Jesus taught us that we cannot "serve two masters, for either he will hate the one and love the other, or he will be devoted to the one and despise the other. You cannot serve both God and mammon." He goes on to elaborate that we shouldn't be anxious about our lives, what we wear, eat, and drink because He will provide all of these when we seek first His kingdom and His righteousness[1].

Maybe you're thinking, "Yeah, I believe that but what does that have to do with being content in my marriage?"

It has a ton to do with being content in your marriage! The lack of contentment leads to anxiety in any area of our lives. If you read what Matthew records in those verses in today's speech, Jesus is saying, "You know what? If you just focus on me and what I do and say, and realize that I'm all you need, not a new car, more money, or a new spouse, then all of things will be given to you as well."

If we pursue God first and only, everything else we need and desire will fall into place and they won't possess and control us or cause anxiety or fear or strongholds. I like what the Apostle Paul says in Philippians 4:11-13:

*Not that I'm speaking of being in need, for I have
learned in whatever situation I am, to be content.
I know how to be brought low and I know how to
abound. In any and every circumstance I have
learned the secret of facing plenty and hunger,
abundance, and need. I can do all things through
Him who strengthens me.*

WHAT'S YOUR SOURCE?

Here's a thought. Don't think about your marriage right now. Beyond with yourself, what gives you a sense of satisfaction and security? Is it your job? Is it your spouse? Is it your friends? Is it your 401(k)? Is it that big bonus you're expecting to get the end of the year? Is it the future that you're on track to attain?

Whatever that is for you, think about it. This should make you feel good. Now, how would you feel or how would your mood shift if that thing or that person or that expectation was gone? Would that devastate you? Would that leave you feeling fearful, unworthy, anxious, depressed, frustrated?

In the 1920s, there was a huge stock market crash. And because things got so bad during that time, people became extremely fearful and depressed. This is why in New York City today, you can no longer open windows on the skyscrapers Or high-rise buildings. And it's all because of the crash in the stock market on Wall Street during that time.

People were jumping out of windows because they felt like that was the only solution to their pain. People were literally jumping to their deaths because their money was gone. So let's go back to that one thing that one person or that one hopeful expectation and future that you are thinking on that brought you a lot of joy.

If that was gone or taken from you, how would you feel? If we're truly pursuing God and nothing else, we'll be disappointed but it won't devastate our lives. It causes a constant friction between people of corrupt mind, who have been robbed of the truth and who think godliness and happiness is a means to financial gain[2]. But Paul teaches us that...

> ...*Godliness with contentment is great gain. For we
> brought nothing into the world, and we can take
> nothing out of it. But if we have food and clothing,
> we will be content with that. Those who want to
> get rich fall into temptation and a trap and into
> many foolish and harmful desires that plunge
> people into ruin and destruction. For the love of
> money is a root of all kinds of evil. Some people,
> eager for money, have wandered from the faith and
> pierced themselves with many griefs. But you,
> man of God, flee from all this, and pursue
> righteousness, godliness, faith, love, endurance
> and gentleness[3].*

Paul isn't saying we must be poor to be content. He doesn't say that money is the root of all evil. The love of it is. What really stood out to me in this passage was that if you're not content, it'll lead to an ungodly life. You'll begin to desire things that are not what God wants for you.

Our relationship with God should be our source of contentment. Hebrews 13:5-6 says,

> *Keep your lives free from the love of money and be
> content with what you have, because God has said,
> "Never will I leave you; never will I forsake you."
> So we say with confidence,
> "The Lord is my helper; I will not be afraid. What can
> mere mortals do to me?*

If you suffer from anxiety, examine where your focus lies. Are you focused on God and His thoughts and His ways, or are you pursuing something else for selfish reasons? If God is for us, that should keep us content by itself. This has nothing to do with your marriage right now, but everything to do with you as a person.

Are you a contented person? I'll be transparent with you here. I struggle with this in my life. I am the stereotypical American through and through. I suffer with materialism. I love to buy things. I grow tired or complacent with things and want to get more or something new.

If you know me, you know that I love cars. And what's sad is that I love all cars but the one I have. And the sadder thing is, when I get a new one, I lose my excitement for that one too. Every time I say, "Oh, I'm going to love this for a long time" and get it, it loses its attractiveness to me.

This is not okay and will spill over into my marriage if I don't take it captive and hold it against God's word.

CONTENTMENT IN YOUR MARRIAGE

To be content simply means to be mentally and emotionally satisfied with the way things are. Someone who is content is willing to accept the current circumstances with peace and light.

Now don't get me wrong, our goal is to make our marriages better.

If you're at a zero, let's get you to at least a one or two to give you momentum. If you're a seven, let's get you to a nine.

So the goal is to make our lives and our marriages and our relationships stronger and better. There's a fine line between better and not being happy with your marriage. If you find yourself constantly saying things like, "I wish he or she would do this" or "I wish he or she would do this" then your radar should be up.

People who are discontent in their marriages, usually make themselves and their spouses miserable. Take a close and honest look at yourself. Are you content in your marriage? Are you making your marriage better or worse? And if you are content in your marriage, who is the first person that's going to notice it? Your spouse.

Your spouse knows you best. They know what you're thinking. They know when you come home from work whether you had a good day or bad day.

Rhonda always says, "How's your day?" If I don't respond or ask her the same when I walk in, she immediately knows what kind of a day I had. Spouses know each other. If you hang around someone long enough, you'll start to notice these things as well. It's just part of marriage and close relationships.

People who are discontent are never satisfied. They always want more, expect more, and demand more. Instead of recognizing the positive aspects of their spouse, they focus on the negatives. Where they could build up their spouse with words of encouragement and appreciation, they instead, tear them down with criticism, resentment, or passive comments. You cannot be discontent in your marriage and have a forever marriage. It just doesn't work.

8 TIPS TO DEVELOP CONTENTMENT IN YOUR MARRIAGE

I'll share with you eight perspectives that'll help you keep the right focus and attention on your spouse. If you follow these eight things, your marriage will become a forever marriage and others will learn from you.

- *Realize that no one is perfect—including you.*

You might have just cheered or said, "Amen" at that. But here's the thing, we're not saying, "I'm not perfect, so you need to accept that." What we're saying is that we need to realize our spouse is not perfect and show them grace.

If you've been married longer than a day, you probably have

already noticed your spouse is no saint. And before you get on your high horse, neither are you. I know I'm not!

Marriage is the joining of two imperfect people, committed to helping the other get stronger together. It's easy to get an unhealthy view of these imperfections and think, "Her problems are worse than mine. I'm closer to perfect than she is."

This may be true, but if you're thinking that way in a self-righteous kind of way, then *check yourself before you wreck yourself.*

One of my favorite songs that convicts me to the core is the song *Broken Together* by Casting Crowns. The lyrics are haunting to me as a reminder to cherish my wife, and that we're both broken without Jesus.

The words go like this...

What do you think about when you look at me
I know we're not the fairy tale you dreamed we'd be
You wore the veil, you walked the aisle, you took my hand And
we dove into a mystery
How I wish we could go back to simpler times
Before all our scars and all our secrets were in the light Now
on this hallowed ground, we've drawn the battle lines Will we
make it through the night?
It's going to take much more than promises this time Only God
can change our minds
Maybe you and I were never meant to be complete Could we
just be broken together.
If you can bring your shattered dreams and I'll bring mine
Could healing still be spoken and save us
The only way we'll last forever is broken together How it must
have been so lonely by my side
We were building kingdoms and chasing dreams and left love
behind
I'm praying God will help our broken hearts align And we
won't give up the fight

It's going to take much more than promises this time Only God can change our minds
Maybe you and I were never meant to be complete Could we just be broken together
If you can bring your shattered dreams and I'll bring mine
Could healing still be spoken and save us
The only way we'll last forever is broken together Maybe you and I were never meant to be complete Could we just be broken together
If you can bring your shattered dreams and I'll bring mine
Could healing still be spoken and save us
The only way we'll last forever is broken together

The song talks about how she wanted to marry a Prince when she was a little girl. He wanted a beautiful bride. And all of a sudden, they're married and saying, "This isn't what we signed up for!" And then it goes on to say, "Why can't we just be broken together?"

That's what I want for you to take away from this. You and your spouse are both broken pieces of clay that the master sculptor (Jesus) can mold into beautiful vessels. The key to a forever marriage is accepting your spouse as imperfect, cherishing and focusing on their strengths, and speaking to those.

YOUR SPOUSE WILL HURT YOU

I'll make one promise to you about your marriage. Your spouse is going to disappoint you. He's going to hurt you, discourage you, shame you, belittle you, curse you, and treat you in every way and form that he shouldn't and that you don't deserve. But you know what's also true? You will too.

That's just life when you have two broken people living and doing life together. It's inevitable unless we bring God into the center of our relationship. We're human. We're selfish by nature and instinct. We'll talk more about unselfishness in *Chapter 6*.

- *You can't control your spouse.*

You can't control her no matter how good you think you can fix her.

You can't control him no matter how good you think you can train him.

No matter how righteous or perfect you think you are, you're not the Holy Spirit. We cannot change our mate. Think about that for a moment. Doesn't that remove the burden off of you? You aren't responsible for fixing them. So what does this really mean? Who can change your spouse then? The Holy Spirit. What's the best way to help them? Pray for them.

We must be cautious with our prayers as well. If we're praying for God to have them do everything we want and tell them to do, that's selfish. We want to be sure we're asking God to change their heart and their desires to be more like Him, and as a by-product of that, they'll treat us better.

Have you ever noticed that when you try to fix, change, correct, or train your spouse, they become resistant, defensive, and turn away? It's our nature to flee from danger or uncomfortable situations. If you're constantly attacking your spouse, they will shut down and withdraw. This is a recipe for disaster.

- *You can only change yourself.*

If there's something in your marriage you don't like or your spouse does or won't do something you want, the only way to change them and improve the situation is change the part that you can control: you.

This is a big deal. When Rhonda and I counsel couples, we often have each spouse come to us saying, "I keep telling him that if he would just do this or stop doing that…" or "If she would just change and do this…" our marriage would be great.

And we say, "Look, stop trying to change them and control the situation. The only thing you can change and control is yourself."

But this is really hard to do, especially in the heat of battle. We're selfish by nature and this doesn't come naturally. We must work at it and make a deliberate choice to work on ourselves. This is even harder when your spouse may be the one who is the majority of the problem and refuses to acknowledge this and take full responsibility. This is compounded when you don't see immediate results or improvements.

Instead of saying, "I want mine and you need to change so I can get mine," we should draw a circle around ourselves and say, "I'll change everything inside this circle because it's within my control to do so."

We've counseled many couples where each one is blaming the other spouse saying, "It's 100% his or her fault." Now, I will say, there have been some times where one of the spouses was mostly at fault. Usually when this happens, the one who has the most work to do is blaming the one with the least.

Change yourself, change your marriage. Focus on the good things. Why not try saying something like, "My husband is a great provider." "My wife is an excellent mother to our children." Focus on what they're good at, not what they lack. Right now, if you just got married and everything is going well, this is easy.

"Yeah, she's everything I've ever wanted."

"He's the perfect husband I've always dreamed of."

If that's you, great! Remember how that feels and continue to treat your spouse that way. For everyone else not quite there yet or who has lost touch with that lovey-dovey feeling, we got to work on it.

"But, Biff. I do praise my spouse."

Yeah, but are you vocalizing it to them? If you're telling others or keeping it inside your head, that's not helping your spouse. They need to hear it and hear it constantly. And by you speaking it out loud, it actually alters your perception and emotions toward them.

FIND THE POSITIVE AND STICK WITH IT

You got to find something to be grateful for. The thing is, there should be a list of things you like about your spouse. No matter how bad it may seem in the moment, they're the same person you fell in love with and married, they just may have lost their way (and potentially due to you forgetting yourself).

One of the activities Rhonda and I like doing with couples when we counsel them is have them list out loud the qualities that attracted them to their spouses when they first started dating and got married.

Usually, it takes them a bit to think about it. You see, there's so much we take for granted every day that we forget how awesome our spouses have always been. If I become angry because the food wasn't hot at dinner, that's silly and foolish.

It's hard to remember our spouses in a positive light when things are rough, especially things outside of your control like finances and work. It's equally as challenging when you have the thought of, "What if I change but they don't?" Or, "If I change, what will change about them?"

The key is to remember to always surrender to God and let him fill you and change your spouse. If you keep your eyes on Him, you'll never see the shortcomings of your spouse, only the beauty inside of them.

- *Walk in gratitude.*

There is a lot to be thankful for. Find something and think on it. Focus on what you have, not what you don't have. Scripture reminds us repetitively to be grateful and thankful.

Be thankful for your marriage.

Be thankful that your spouse is employed. Be thankful your children are healthy.

Be thankful you have a good relationship with your in-laws or parents.

- *Brag on your spouse's good points.*

Don't just think it or tell others, share it out loud with your spouse. When you say things out loud that your spouse is good at, it becomes what you focus on. Don't assume your husband knows you're proud of him. Tell him constantly and every day. Don't assume your wife knows you think she's the most beautiful person on the planet and you couldn't be more thankful for a better mother to your children. Tell her every day outwardly.

I've had some business issues the last few months and the other day Rhonda and I were in the store. I was feeling down and I had just been hammered with some bad news with a deal. It was one thing after the next in my business that just kept happening and had me worried.

She noticed something was wrong and came over and put her hand on my shoulder and said, "I just want you to know, I'm proud of you."

And of course, since I was having a pity-party, I responded with some childish remark because I was hurting. And she just repeated, "I'm proud of you because of the man you are, not when things are going well, but when things aren't going so well."

Because she knew me and chose to focus on my strengths and that we were a team, she reminded me of what I was good at and why she loved me. That helped pull me out of that funk and fill me with courage and strength. This is what the Bible means when it says for wives to be humble and meek. A woman has incredible power over a man. She can either utterly destroy him with her words and actions, or create a king out of him.

BE SPECIFIC WITH YOUR PRAISE

We attend Champion Forest Baptist Church and the pastor for over thirty years, Damon Shook, used to say, "If you come up to me after the sermon and say, 'That was a good sermon' why don't you, instead, come up and say, 'That was a good sermon because it ministered to me and encouraged me to not give up on God's promises for my marriage.'"

When you say something positive to your spouse, be specific. When I was done because of business, Rhonda knew it and tried to encourage me by telling me she was proud of me. But then she realized she needed to go deeper with specifics. It was those details that broke me out of my funk and made me feel supported.

If you work on your marriage, things will change. Over thirty years ago when Rhonda and I first started dating and got married, she wouldn't have said those encouraging words to me. Not because she didn't believe them, but because she struggled in this area. She was quiet, even more than she is now. Words of affirmation were not her strength. However, it's a need of mine and she grew into that to meet my need.

What used to be a weakness of hers is now one of her greatest strengths. This goes back to changing yourself. Change yourself for the need of your husband or your wife. If you do, marriage can do some incredible things.

- *Get rid of negative influences.*

We've mentioned Hallmark movies earlier and those are a great example of how to treat your spouse with kindness. The issue is that it can set comparative examples of how spouses treat each other that may be unfair. Now, I'm not saying that when you're going home with your wife you say, "See! You shouldn't be watching those movies!"

What I'm saying ladies (since most women are the ones who

would watch Hallmark) is that if you see or hear something that makes you go, "Oh, I wish he was that way." Then stop watching those shows, movies, or spending time with those people.

I'm not saying get rid of positive influences that show you what life could be like, I'm saying to remove those things that make you feel resentment toward your spouse or envy toward someone else that isn't your spouse. Likewise, if there's something or someone influencing you to leave your spouse or treat them harshly, flee from it!

Get rid of all negative influences from your life. Even if a movie or show or friend isn't directly saying anything negative about their spouse or yours, if it's full of cursing, sex, slander, greed, violence, or does not build up in a godly way, it'll contaminate your marriage through your thoughts and will lead to discontentment.

- *Spend time in prayer for your marriage.*

This is often seen as a cliché response, and often powerless, but it's the most powerful and important thing you can do for your spouse, your marriage, and for others.

Ask the Lord to give you a fresh passion for your spouse, daily. Ask Him to remind you of your spouse's strengths. Spend time in prayer *for* your spouse, not *about* your spouse. Also, pray and ask God to help you become the best husband or wife for your spouse. Ask Him to use you to be everything your spouse needs and the Holy Spirit to quicken in your heart and mind all of the strengths about your spouse.

Pray that you'll be blinded to their weaknesses. That's a big one. If you no longer see your spouse's weaknesses or faults, you'll cherish them completely. And as a result, they will respond in kind to you.

YOUR MARRIAGE CAN THRIVE

You don't need to be perfect in marriage to be content. There's no such thing. They're not perfect, and you're not perfect. But, you can have a perfectly imperfect marriage by focusing on your spouse's strengths and needs.

This leads to contentment. Your marriage doesn't have to be perfect to be content. You only need to change your mindset and thoughts to create it.

If you find yourself praying about your spouse and asking God to change them, then you know right away that you're seeking contentment in your spouse (who is flawed) and this is a recipe for disappointment because God is the only true source for our needs.

There are three people in a marriage, not two. You, your spouse, and God. Or, another way to say it is you, your spouse, and your marriage. My contentment isn't in Rhonda, it's in our marriage, which comes from God.

Start with counting the blessings in your marriage and don't take them for granted. Marriage is a great thing. If you've ever been lonely or single for awhile and wanting to find someone to love you, you'll see just how awesome marriage is for the human spirit.

WE'RE BETTER TOGETHER

"Two are better than one because they have a good reward for their toil.[4]"

There's a reason Rhonda and I were called to lead a young married couples life group and not a singles ministry. Marriage is the first thing God created with man. God created this union between a male and female to showcase His goodness and image.

If you're not in a good place right now in your marriage, take heart. Use what I share in this book and you will win your spouse back and have a powerful marriage that changes the world around you.

Just remember, if you've ever gone to the gym and worked out, you don't see results right away. It takes a daily commitment to keep putting in the world before results show up, and when they do, they begin to compound and go faster. Also, I never say, "I wish I hadn't gone to the gym today." It's the same with your marriage.

Doing the right thing is always the right thing and will reap a harvest if you don't give up or lose hope. Fight for your marriage. Fight to be content in your marriage.

I like this saying I heard, "When you're having trouble with your marriage, think back to when all you wanted is what you got."

CONTENTMENT RECAP

- Contentment is a mindset and belief.
- Contentment is not having the things you want, but wanting the things you have.
- Comparison will divide your marriage. Envy will pollute your marriage.
- Negative thoughts and influences will contaminate your thoughts and opinions toward your spouse and your marriage. Get rid of them.
- No one is perfect.
- Show grace to your spouse.
- Think only of the positives and good things about your spouse and speak them out loud to them regularly.
- You're stronger together, not apart.

LOVE IN ACTION

- Write down what you wish your marriage looked like. Why do you desire that?
- What can you do to help get your marriage to where you want it to be?
- In what ways do you wish your spouse would change or improve?

- How can you change or improve yourself to make your marriage stronger?
- What are your spouses needs?
- What can you do to show your spouse you care?

———————————————

1. Matthew 6:24-33
2. 1 Timothy 6:5
3. 1 Timothy 6:6-11
4. Ecclesiastes 4:9

5

SPIRITUALITY

Spirituality in marriage is crucial. Without God holding two people together, there's no hope for them to succeed. When I say spirituality, I don't mean attending church. It's much more than going to church on Wednesdays and Sundays or celebrating religious holidays and traditions. However, we will see that certain religious dominations have lower divorce rates than others.

DIVORCE RATE BASED ON DOMINATION

We've already covered that the national average in America for divorce is 49%. This holds true for marriages inside and outside of the church. But is it the same among the different denominations in Christianity?

Let's look at the top ones.

- Catholics are 31% less likely to get divorced.
- Protestants are 35% less likely to get divorced.
- Jews are 97% less likely to get divorced.

We see about the same among the two main dominations in Christianity, but Judaism really skyrockets. Why do you think that is? Here are a few of the reasons I believe we find a much lower divorce rate among the Jewish faith.

- They follow the Old Testament Law.
- Restrictions on divorce are steep.
- The husband must give his wife a divorce document.
- Marriage ends only if one of the spouses dies.
- Marriage is a covenant bond and a man and woman become one flesh.

One way to look at this wide gap is how in Judaism their faith really solidifies their marriage. While Jews don't believe Jesus Christ was the Messiah, they still believe and hold fast to the Old Testament in the Bible. There are different groups within Judaism, but as a whole, practicing Jews are pretty religious and traditional.

Interestingly enough, when we branch deeper into the different denominations among the Protestant groups, we find that Conservative Protestants are less likely to get divorced than the Protestant group as a whole.

Why is that? Perhaps it's they're more gracious or liberal in their beliefs. But one thing that sticks out to me is the idea of transparency versus masks. When we're around our church friends, when we're at church, it's easy to say, "Hey, how's it going?"

"I'M FINE" IS A CRY FOR HELP

The last time you went to church or you saw someone and they asked you how you were, what did you say? Did you say, "Hey, I'm doing great!" But were you really doing great? You don't need to answer that as I'm not asking for you to air your dirty laundry, but just think on that for a bit. We are so used to putting on a facade that all is fantastic in our lives due to social media. Or, we go to the opposite extreme and use victimhood as a badge of honor. Neither is healthy.

Many times in a more liberal setting, there are less masks. People are more open and direct with their real issues, some more than others who do it for attention. In conservative churches, the notion is we're all supposed to be doing great. Isn't that what happens when you become a believer? Everything goes smoothly?

You might laugh but many people believe that and it's what has caused many believers to fall away from their faith.

If someone were to ask me how I was doing and I gave the generic and kosher response of, "I'm doing well. Thank you." And then leave church, get in the truck with Rhonda, and pick up where I left off before we got to church and started cursing her out, what would that make me? A hypocrite would be a light way to say it.

What about if the opposite happened? I asked several others and they all gave me the "I'm great!" Response and I go back in the truck with Rhonda and think to myself, "Man, we must be pretty messed up because everyone else has no problems and life is perfect for them. What's wrong with me?" Or, if I was being selfish, "What's wrong with Rhonda! I need a new wife."

See the danger here when we're not honest? It opens up a tidal wave of masked perfection or overt insecurities through victimhood. In both cases, comparison and a lack of honesty is the root cause that bleeds into other areas of our lives. And if left unkept, we'll contaminate our marriage.

Now, I must caution. I'm not saying to be the biggest downer and pity-partier that shows up to church or when you meet up with your friends, family, or a stranger asks you at the grocery store and say, "Man, he was such a jerk this morning." Or "She was so late! She can't even get somewhere on time." If things aren't great, just say, "Not great." And tell them how they can pray for you.

The study found that Nominal Conservative Protestants (those who rarely worship and consider themselves conservative) had a higher rate.

This is why the divorce rate is the same inside the church as the secular world. It's not because spirituality can't save marriages, because it absolutely can and will. It's because people aren't living out what they say they believe or doing what God teaches.

Now, there's a tiny fraction of situations where divorce might be the only viable option. But it's rare. God wants us together, not apart.

WHAT DOES THE BIBLE SAY ABOUT SPIRITUALITY?

Here's the tricky part. You've got to realize that spirituality is an individual thing. It doesn't matter how spiritual your spouse is, you are responsible for your own faith.

So if your spouse is extremely spiritual but you don't believe in God, you're still on your way to hell despite their belief if you don't have a personal relationship with Jesus Christ.

It doesn't matter how often or how many times your spouse prays with you, for you, or about you. If you don't know Jesus Christ as your Lord and Savior, then narrow is the way.

Faith or spirituality is individual. Notice, I didn't say *personal* because your faith should be personal *and* shared with others. This is also true for the spouse who is a believer. Your faith will not save your spouse no matter how hard you try.

But what does God say about both spouses being spiritually in-tune? The Bible has a lot to stay about being likeminded in Christ. Let's look at a few verses that stood out to me.

> "Let the Word of Christ dwell in you richly, reaching
> and admonishing one another in all wisdom,
> singing songs and hymns and spiritual songs with
> thankfulness in your hearts to God.[1]"

Paul says we should be together, sing together, learn together, study together, do life together.

"Not neglecting the fellowship of believers, as is the
habit of some, but encouraging one another, and
all the more as you see the Day drawing near.[2]"

In other words, build up and correct other believers when they're
gone astray or are down, and don't go too far without help.

"Addressing one another in psalms and hymns and
spiritual songs, singing in humility to the Lord
with your heart.[3]"

Notice how these verses aren't singular, they're speaking to all of
us as one body; togetherness. Now maybe you're asking whether that
pertains to your spouse also. If not them, then who? There's no question
that it also speaks to our spouses.

We know God ordained marriage and He also ordained the
church. So, of course He means your spouse as well. What does the
Bible say about the power of connecting spiritually?

"For where two or three are gathered in my name,
there I am among them.[4]"

Earlier in the chapter, Matthew writes, *"But first, seek the
kingdom of God and His righteousness, and all these things will be
added to you.[5]"*

If you remember from before, the "all these things" refers to
our needs: food, drink, and clothing. So, first off, we must be
connected to the source of spiritual power: God. Once we're
connected with God, we're able to connect in a harmonious
manner with other believers. In marriage, intertwining spirituality
is more than just attending church. Statistically, you should attend
as divorce rates among regular church attendees (those who attend
at least twice a month) is much lower. If you want to have a higher
likelihood of having a forever marriage, join a church and attend

every week. And just like attending church doesn't save you, it doesn't make your marriage spiritual, but it does lead in the right direction.

THE 4 BALANCES OF SPIRITUALITY

These represent four reminders we can leverage to build spirituality in our marriages. These act as guideposts and actions to do to encourage a strong marital bond with our spouses. Before we dive into these four balances, remember that it's crucial and necessary to have spirituality in our marriages if we wish to create, develop, and live out a forever marriage.

- *Church*

We touched on this briefly already but let's go deeper. Keep in mind that going to church does not make you spiritual. However, regular church attendance is the right step in a positive direction toward a strong and spiritual marriage.

Psalms 133:1 says, "*Behold, how good and pleasant it is when brothers dwell in unison.*"

God wants unity with people, especially his people (believers). When we join together at church, we welcome the manifest presence of the Holy Spirit with us. This is why if you've ever been at worship and you suddenly felt an overwhelming sensation of peace, power, love, and emotion during a song, it is the presence of the Holy Spirit with us.

God has three ways we can experience His glory: His internal presence (Holy Spirit within us), omnipresence (His providence in all things), and His manifest presence (during global worship).

One of mine and Rhonda's greatest joys with our married couples life group we lead at Champion Forest Baptist Church is to see couples who when they first started attending the class, were not coming to church regularly. They would confess to me that they'd come every once in awhile. They never attended on a consistent basis. But now, they come every Sunday.

This could be because they made new friends and they sit together or this is where their friends are on Sundays. It could be because my teachings are just out of this world and they walk away every Sunday blown away by the breakthroughs they experienced because of my elegant speech (obviously I'm kidding!).

But the truth is, no matter the reason, they now make it a habit. Now understand what I mean here. You could come to church your whole life and never have a relationship with Jesus Christ. If you have to choose between coming to church but not knowing Jesus Christ as your Lord and Savior or not coming to church and knowing Him personally, don't come to church and choose Jesus Christ every single time.

Now, naturally, if you do know Jesus Christ as your personal Lord and Savior, you'll be convicted (encouraged and challenged) to attend a local church body so that you can be fed God's word and grow in His goodness to bear much fruit for His kingdom.

If you have an intimate relationship with God, you'll desire to come to church because you'll want to worship and be with other likeminded believers.

HABITS

I bet most of you reading this right now have a job, or had a job, or hope to have one soon. And I could wager that each of you has developed a habit of going to work. If tomorrow morning were Monday, you'd probably set your alarm the night before and wake up the following morning when it went off. You have the habit of getting up, getting ready, commuting to work, and working. And the reason why you set your alarm is because you have to get to work by a specific time. If didn't come, or you slacked in your daily work duties, you wouldn't be there long.

It's the same with going to church. When I was young, you didn't come to church only on Sunday mornings. You came Sunday morning, Sunday night, and Wednesday night. There are still these sermon times, but the only difference back then was, everyone went.

Now I'm really going to age myself. We used to have these things called *revivals*. You might want to jot that down. This will blow you away. Sometimes, these revivals would last for up to seven days in a row.

If you're unfamiliar with what a revival is, it's where every night you go to church and hear preaching. We didn't have a band, so we played the piano or organ or something like hat. We'd sing songs that were really, really old. Older than me. I know, that's hard to believe.

But people were in the habit of coming to these revivals, no matter how long they lasted, because they had developed that habit and mindset to go for their benefit. While as a young boy I sometimes dreaded those revival moments, I miss them.

The church today is severely lacking the power and fervor that it once had. Nowadays, we've loosened church. It's harder for people to develop a habit when they only attend maybe once a week, and harder yet, when you attend once a month. That's not a habit. That's just something to do like going to a restaurant or a drive-thru window for fast food.

What about smartphones? They are so smart now. You know what's really cool, is that when I get in my truck every Sunday morning, my phone pops up with the quickest route and time to church. It tells me how long it'll take to get to church and which route is best to get there the fastest. Do you know why it does that? Because I go every Sunday. It knows it's one of my habitual paths.

What's equally impressive, and a bit sad, is that it'll also tell me how long it'll take to get to the golf course. Maybe I play golf too much, or not enough. The point is, your phone remembers where you've been and how often you've been there and on what days. It remembers your consistent and regular routine.

So church is one of our spiritual balances and reminders, but what do you get out of church? One is spiritual learning. When you come to church, you learn about God, what He says about you, what He's called you to do and be in the world, and you receive a word from God that equips you, builds you up, and encourages you so you can go out into your mission field and change lives.

As believers, we need constant fellowship with other believers and to receive God's word and teaching to flood our hearts and minds with His truth so that we may not stumble or be defeated in battle.

Then there's corporate worship. We're with brothers and sisters in Christ praising God together. While this doesn't save you, one thing the Bible makes clear is that it pleases God tremendously to see his children in global worship together, in unity.

This is why small groups or life groups were formed in churches, especially bigger ones. This allows people to be with other like-minded believers to do life together. This is how God planned for it to function. It's a beautiful thing to see fellow believers hanging out at each other's homes, barbecuing hot dogs, burgers, steaks, while the kids run around in the yard, and each person asking how the other is doing in their marriage, life, work, and so forth.

Not neglecting to meet together, as is the habit of some, but encouraging one another, and all the more as you see the Day draw near.

We see even here in Hebrews, God reminding us to not neglect (or stop) meeting together and doing life together. I like how it says, *"habit"* there as well, meaning it can be a habit to join together or to choose not to socialize. And the purpose of doing life together is to *encourage one another as the Day* (when Jesus Christ returns) *approaches.* Isn't that awesome!

WE WERE MADE FOR COMMUNITY

I have a friend named Jeff. He and I went to college together. Jeff has two failed marriages. I'm not sharing anything I wouldn't share if he were present, so don't worry. I love Jeff with every morsel of my soul.

His first marriage lasted for twenty years. Pretty good, right?

FOREVER MARRIAGE

Except, it still ended and was not a forever marriage. He has four children from that marriage. Awhile back he shared something with me that really shook me to my core. It made me really double down on this marriage ministry that Rhonda and I are so passionate about.

He said, "Biff, if we would have been a part of a class like yours (he was referring to soulmates life group at Champion Forest Baptist Church that we lead), we wouldn't have gotten divorced. Here's why," he went on to elaborate. "Because we did it alone. We went through our struggles alone and we had no one to bounce anything off of. That's why we made so many errors. If we would have had people come alongside us, or if we would have gone to someone and said, 'We're struggling with this, can you help us? Or, she's being unfair here with what she's doing or saying, can you offer some guidance?' I know we would have gotten through it and we'd still be married to this day."

Isn't that powerful? They would have celebrated their 35th anniversary this year (2019) if they had stayed together. He told me the other day that they still talk to each other and here's what they told each other.

He told her, "I'm not in love with you, but I still love you."

And she said, "I love you too, Jeff. I know we should have made this work."

That's bittersweet, isn't it? It's beautiful to see they understand it now, but sad that it's too late. Now, go back to what he said before. It would have worked (they never would have divorced or given up on their marriage), not if they had gone to see a counselor or a marriage retreat that resolved their conflicts and differences or studied Francis Chan.

No, he said their marriage would have been saved and prospered if they had a group like the one we have in our married couples group at church. This is why it's vital for the health and well-being of every believer (whether single or married) to attend church every week. We need the fellowship and encouragement of other believers.

The devil wants to get us alone and secluded. That's where he is able to devour us and destroy us. He'd like nothing more to do than to completely annihilate your marriage and shatter your kids' lives through divorce. This is why it's important and life-preserving for you and your spouse to be with other believers on a regular basis. Don't do life alone. Don't do marriage alone. Join others and watch your marriage thrive.

One of our couples' wives said one day in life group that she'd never forget when the class hosted a baby shower for her when she was pregnant with her son. They had just moved to the area and they found out they were pregnant the following month. She said just being able to talk to the other ladies about marriage and pregnancy, to realize she's not a freak, not crazy, and that everything happening between her and her husband was normal. Everyone shared their experience and it encouraged her.

Coming to church isn't always for some deep revelation. It can be as simple as connecting with other wives or husbands and sharing how your husband leaves dishes in the sink and you wish he'd put them in the dishwasher, and then you discover you're not the only one dealing with that. Other husbands fail to do this simple task too.

Church is about connecting, and that's what's missing in society today. We need each other more than ever.

- *Prayer*

Do you and your spouse pray together? This could be before meals or together during the day or before you go to sleep. If you don't, you should start. But don't feel bad, if you do pray with your spouse, you're in the minority.

Praying together is a must to have a spiritual marriage. Maybe you're like some and you think your faith is private and just between you and God. This is not scriptural and it's important you share it with your spouse and discuss together. But if praying together sounds foreign or a bit scary or uncomfortable, then simply start by praying together over your dinner.

Now, I'll share a bonus secret here. Did you know that the Bible never says it's a requirement to pray before every meal? It may surprise you if you were raised in a family like I was where we prayed before every meal. If you took a bite before we prayed, you were on your way to hell.

I'm just teasing. That's not scriptural. But praying before every meal was extremely important, and it still is. I encourage you to start doing this. If you go to lunch today or you're sitting down about to eat dinner, just ask your spouse, "Can we pray?" And if they don't want to lead, then you do.

START WITH A MEAL

Today, I'm meeting up with a friend and will grab something to eat before meeting him. I'll probably get a sub from Subway. What's wrong with me taking a moment to pray before eating? It doesn't require much time to do so, but it shows God I'm thankful for His provision. Just say something like,

> *Thank you, Father, so much for today. Thank you for my class. Thank you for my friends. Thank you for my family. I have a lot to be thankful for.*

> *And thank you for this meal. In Jesus' name. Amen.*

See how simple that is? You don't have to know everything about the Bible to pray or be some theologian and know specific words. Just talk to God like you would a friend.

If you want to make a fun game out of it, try doing this with your family (especially if you have children). Make it to where the last person to put their finger on their nose has to pray for the meal. You can play little games like this to teach your kids it's important to pray and thank God for what He's given you. It's great to teach your kids how to pray and the importance of prayer. Even if it seems like a punishment at first, it's still developing a solid habit for them that will serve them in the years to come.

So, if you're not praying yet, start by praying together at meals then work up to praying with your spouse over your marriage, family, dreams, hopes, fears, desires, goals, and vision. A good way to do this is three times per day, you know, each time you eat.

If you only eat one meal (dinner) with your spouse, then start there. And as you go, start to incorporate more into your prayers than just thanking God for the food. You'll begin to share things about your spouse, your children, your work day, your environment and society, and so forth. It'll build your faith.

For Rhonda and me, I usually pray, but sometimes she will. And when she does, it's beautiful. It's not some 20-minute prayer, but just being raw and real with each other and with God. We'll pray for our children. We'll pray for our grandchildren. We'll pray for our class. And we pray for specific issues that friends or people we know are going through. Praying at your meals is the starting point to build a new and positive habit for prayer.

As you mature in this area and grow into it, you'll begin to incorporate prayer throughout your day. And when you do this, you'll start to see your life and then lives of those around you supernaturally transform.

It'll become easy to pray with your spouse. Imagine what it would be like if your spouse had a loved one, a sibling or parent or dear friend, who found out they had a terminal illness, and they found out about it today.

How easy would it be for you to stop what you were doing and pray with them? Would you stop and ask them, "Let's pray?" Would that be natural for you? Would you think to do it?

If that's not natural or an instinctive response throughout your day and situations, then it's key you start small (praying at meals) and work up to praying for every situation and circumstance (big and small) to build that muscle.

WHERE TWO OR THREE AGREE...

To encourage you, I want to share what 1 John 5:14-15 says we gain from prayer:

> This is the confidence that we have toward Him, that
> if we ask anything according to His will, He hears
> us. If we know that He hears us, then whatever
> we ask, we know that we have the request that we
> have asked of Him.

The Bible tells us that if two or three agree on anything, the Father who is in heaven, hears them and will give them anything that they ask. When you're together and you pray together, and you agree on it, God hears you and will answer your request. This is why corporate prayer (corporate includes you and your spouse) is so powerful and vital to the well-being of the church and the world.

God hears you no matter what, but start praying together as a family, as a couple. When you do, you will see the windows of heaven open up in your life and marriage and the supernatural manifested. Ask for things in agreement and together, and see it happen.

> Whatever you do in word or deed, do everything in
> the name of the Lord Jesus, giving thanks to God
> the Father through Him[6].

This is a great reminder for us to keep at the forefront of our minds. We pray because we're grateful for what God has done for us and given us. Start with meals and work up to praying throughout the day.

Pray for your meal. Pray for your work. Pray for your marriage and your spouse. Pray for your kids. Pray for your health. Pray for your parents and friends. Pray for your neighborhood. Pray for your country. Pray for your faith.

In whatever you do, pray and thank God and you will thrive in your marriage, relationships, and life.

- *Spiritual Conversation*

Do you and your spouse talk about spiritual things? Do you share what God is doing in your life and what He's saying to you? Do you ask your spouse what God is speaking to their heart about?

Does that sound crazy or scary to you? If so, that's good. That means you have a huge potential for growth and supernatural breakthrough waiting for you to tap into. And this may sound even more weird to you, but Rhonda and I do this all of the time.

Out of the all of the marriages out there, I bet you only 30-50% of them do this. If you are one of those who doesn't speak about spiritual things with your spouse, I'm not slamming you. Don't feel discouraged or condemned. Remember, *there is therefore now no condemnation to them which are in Christ Jesus, who walk not after the flesh, but after the Spirit*[7].

Maybe you've been raised to believe, "I have my relationship with Christ and they have their relationship with Christ. My faith is personal to me. I don't need to share it or talk about it with anyone."

If you have a relationship with God, that's great! I would encourage you to share it with your spouse and what God is doing in your life and spiritual walk with Him. If your spouse doesn't do this or is resistant to it, don't worry. You do it, and they will learn from your example and will come around.

LOVE COVERS A MULTITUDE OF SINS

We redeem our spouses and cover a multiple of shortcomings with our love[8]. By you sharing your faith and leading by example, your spouse will have time to grow into it and learn a better way. And when they open up, prepare yourself for the beauty that will radiate in your life.

My mother loves to talk about spiritual things. My father doesn't, until maybe ten years ago. You know what's awesome? To see an older man, who's in his 70s, start talking about spiritual things and for that stronghold you have fallen away. Now, usually we see people turn to God and become super spiritual when they're about to die. Not so with my father. Just one day, he started talking more about spiritual matters.

I don't know why he did, he just did. But I know this, my mom tried her whole life to get him to open up about his faith and spiritual things, and he finally did. This is the power of perseverance. Sometimes it takes several decades for a stronghold to break and for your spouse to finally come around on something, but don't lose heart. Though it may seem like nothing is happening outwardly, we know we're renewed inwardly each day. And any momentary struggle is outweighed by the glory that we'll experience[9].

OUR WORDS SHOULD BUILD UP, NOT TEAR DOWN

Maybe you've heard of the verse,

> Do not let any unwholesome talk come out of your mouths, but only what is helpful for building others up according to their needs, that it may benefit those who listen[10].

What does that mean to you? What do you consider "unwholesome talk"? Is that cursing? Is it passive aggressive comments, joking, sarcasm, crude humor, gestures, rude remarks?

Here's a simple rule of thumb for you. If it's not building someone up, it's unwholesome speech. No matter how good intentioned you may be (or think you're being), if it doesn't encourage someone, build them up, praise them, support them, and bring them hope, it's tearing them down.

The more you have spiritual conversations with your spouse (and with others), the less likely you'll be prone to unwholesome speech and discussions. And the less likely you are to have a poor or bad conversation with your spouse.

It's kind of difficult to say to Rhonda, "Let me tell you what God is doing in my life," and then follow it up with, "And by the way, you burned the roast last night! Where was your mind, woman?"

Those words won't come out of my mouth (or even in my thoughts) if I'm submitted to God, pursing Him daily, and sharing it with my spouse. Yes, we slip up from time to time, but as a whole, it'll be far less frequent or damaging. And we'll be able to show more grace to our spouses (or receive it) when they stumble.

When you're acting spiritual, when you're talking about what God is doing in your life or how you see Him working in it, it's much harder to be critical and ugly and mean to your spouse, to your kids, to others, and to yourself.

> Let your speech always be gracious, seasoned with
> salt, so that you may know how you ought to
> answer each person[11].

I love that verse. It reminds us that we much be mindful of our words, not only what we say, but how we say it. People judge and react to our nonverbal queues more than they do to our actual words.

How do you answer others? I imagine it's largely based on how you're feeling in that moment or where your thoughts are. If you're in a hurry or if your kids are screaming in the backseat, your response may be different than if you were sitting on a quiet beach, listening to the waves crash against the black lava rocks.

But God tells us to season (be careful and attention to) our words as salt (adding flavor or substance to) those around us. If words are an issue in your marriage, then this is a great area to start praying and asking God to reveal His wisdom and insight to you in how to engage with your spouse better in a more loving manner.

Ask God to open up avenues for you to have these spiritual

conversations and watch as your spouse blossoms and your marriage prospers.

- *Living A Spiritual Marriage*

You may be thinking, "Aren't we already talking about that?" Yes, and no. Here's the thing, living a spiritual marriage involves incorporating spiritual things into your daily life. Make your day-to-day activities with your spouse include things of a spiritual nature.

> To set the mind on the flesh is death, but to set the mind on the spirit is life and peace...You, however, are not in the flesh but in the spirit, if in fact the spirit of God dwells in you. Anyone who does not have the spirit of Christ does not belong to Him[12].

What do you think resides in the things of the flesh? What do you think represents the things of the spirit? How could we reduce our fleshy (sinful) side and increase our spirit (righteous) self?

> If we live by the spirit, let us also keep in step with the spirit[13].

It's not enough to have Christ in us, but to live out our lives as Christ would by submitting to the spirit of Christ who dwells within us and letting His ways become our ways, His thoughts our thoughts, His sight our vision, and His speech our tongues.

Spirituality in marriage and living a spiritual life go hand-in-hand. You can't have one without the other or your marriage will be lopsided and your faith void of life. That is why James tells us that faith without works is dead[14]. Just as it is with our faith, a marriage without spirituality and spiritual activities is lifeless.

Going to church is a spiritual activity. But that's surface level and not what I mean by living a spiritual marriage. For example, devotions.

Rhonda and I both have separate devotions we read and study each day. I recommend you and your spouse do that as well. However after you've had a chance to study and read the word alone, come together with your spouse and share your key takeaways that God revealed to you in your devotion.

What's amazing is that God will oftentimes reveal through his word the answers and solutions to what you or your spouse may be going through at that exact moment. By you sharing your devotion with your spouse, you may be delivering their answer to a prayer.

So many times God has spoken to me or to Rhonda on specific things our spouse needed ministered to on. It's amazing how many times God will deposit into your quiet time precisely the words your spouse needs to hear if they're going through a difficult time.

A word of caution. If your spouse is having a difficult time or comes to you about something they're dealing with, don't go, "I have an idea. Why don't you just do this? It'll solve everything!"

Instead, come to them in humility and love and share with your spouse what God has been saying to you and revealing to you through His word. This will bridge the spiritual connection required for our spouses to receive our encouragement without feeling judged, condemned, or critiqued.

Could you imagine having a marriage without sexuality? I could almost hear all of the men yell, "No!" through the digital world and the women say, "Finally!" While there are differences between spousal needs and desires, both parties still need and want sex.

Without it, we miss that deeper and more intimate connection and bond that God created for marriages. And on a more practical side, the human race would go extinct pretty quickly if no one was making babies anymore. You see ladies, God put in man the urge to spread seed to multiply the earth. We're just obeying His command.

Before I get too many fun emails, I'll digress. Just like it's hard to imagine marriage without sex, it's equally as improbable and lifeless to leave our spirituality.

Sex is fleeting. It's pleasureful for a moment then it's done and you move onto the next day, the hunger renewed. With spirituality, however, it's a lifelong journey and part of our lives. It's with us after death and for all eternity.

Do you see the difference and importance between sexuality and spirituality? And yet, many marriages end in divorce because of sexuality. In America, this is a big problem because we're conditioned to believe that if we're not getting what we want that we should get it from someone who is willing to give it. And we completely disregard the spirituality aspect.

SPIRITUALITY BEGINS AS AN INDIVIDUAL THING

Spiritual is an individual thing, but it shouldn't be left out of marriages. Just because your spiritual walk with God depends on your choices, doesn't mean your spouse won't benefit from your faith, and you'll both grow together, faster.

If you're not sharing your faith with your spouse and joining hands in your walk with God, your marriage is lacking the power source. I find it ironic and amazing how super spiritual people still get divorced. It shows me that they weren't living a spiritual marriage.

My mission is to see the national divorce rate go from 49% to 0% with everyone who reads this book. Now, like I mentioned earlier, there are some situations where abuse or drug and alcohol addiction are involved, or something else, and the children or spouse is in danger, and divorce is the only viable option in that moment. But, with those instances aside (and even then), all marriages should have a 100% chance to thrive when they do it God's way. And a key component to that succeeding is spirituality in the marriage.

THE GRASS ISN'T GREENER

Marriage is not for the weak at heart and the easily prone to quit. The grass is never greener on the other side. Every one has their own unique issues that they bring into relationships that each spouse must work to resolve, heal, and build from. And the divorce rate increases dramatically for every time you get a divorce, the odds are not in your favor with your next partner.

It's best to stay with your first and implement the tools and principles I'm sharing in this book to ensure that your marriage thrives and divorce never becomes an option.

PRAYER

Father, thank you so much for today. Thank you for every day that you've blessed us with. Thank you for the church and the body of people you called to you that we might do life together.

Thank you for each person reading this book, Father. Thank you for blessing Rhonda and me with being a part of this mission to see every marriage become a forever marriage.

Father, I pray that you help each of us in our marriages that we make spirituality a crucial part of our lives, and allow for you to be a part of it and move in us, as we become more spiritual and yield and surrender to your will.

I ask you to anoint every marriage, Father. I pray that they will have a wonderful week, and that each day, their marriages will increase and prosper as we watch you work in mysterious ways.

We love you, Father, and we ask these things in Jesus' name. Amen.

SPIRITUALITY RECAP

- National divorce rate is 49%.
- God created marriages for a 100% success rate.
- The rate of divorce reduces depending on the level of spiritual commitment to attend church and religious traditions.
- Transparency is your ally with your spouse. Spirituality is necessary for your marriage to thrive.
- Living a spiritual life enhances and increases your chance for success and a forever marriage.
- The 4 Balances of Spirituality: Church, Prayer, Spiritual Conversation, Living a Spiritual Marriage

LOVE IN ACTION

- Share your true feelings with your spouse, but don't make it a pity-party where you're just complaining and whining. Be sincere with your concerns, fears, doubts, feelings, emotions, hopes, and dreams. Your spouse is there to support you.
- If you don't attend church regularly, find a local church and start going every Sunday.
- If you want to grow in your walk with God faster and deeper, do a devotion and study the Bible every day on your own, and then come together with your spouse to discuss what God is speaking to you.
- Pray with your spouse over your marriage, children, friends, family, career, hopes & dreams, fears & doubts,

and for Him to reveal His will to you through His word. Commit to never divorce.

- If you're struggling in your marriage or want to take it to the next level, connect with other likeminded believers and do life in a community.
- Never quit on yourself or your marriage.

---

1. Colossians 3:16
2. Hebrews 10:25
3. Ephesians 5:18
4. Matthew 18:20
5. Matthew 6:33
6. Colossians 3:17
7. Romans 8:1
8. 1 Peter 4:8
9. 2 Corinthians 4:16-18
10. Ephesians 4:29
11. Colossians 4:6
12. Romans 8:6,9
13. Galatians 5:25
14. James 2:14-26

6

UNSELFISHNESS

Four years ago my uncle had a severe car accident that messed up his back and he had to walk with a cane. However, because he's six feet four inches tall, he doesn't use it (the cane that is). Instead, he uses a walking stick to balance himself or he'll topple over.

He and his wife have been married nearly sixty years and every day she would help him and walk by his side ever since that accident. The level of selfless love for him was intoxicating and palatable.

The other day, his wife, Linda, had a stroke. It was on a Monday morning around five o'clock. Six days later, he still hadn't been home or left her side. As a matter of fact, he refused to go home. His three daughters eventually sent out an email saying, "Dad is finally going home tonight."

That's the kind of bond they had with one another. They exuded the epitome of a forever marriage with how they treated each other, loved each other, and sacrificed for one another. They never gave up or abandoned the other no matter what was going on.

LOVE ENDURES ALL THINGS

The other night, Rhonda and I were at a wedding. It was my nephew's wedding and we got home rather late. It was about midnight if I recall. And we passed by my uncle's house and his Mercedes was in the driveway with the lights still on.

I pulled in without a thought to see how Linda was doing since he hadn't been home for several days. No sooner had I pulled up than his daughter jumped out of the Mercedes and said to me, "He's not here."

"Yeah, but he's coming home, right?" "No," she said. "He won't leave her."

Rhonda and I exchanged looks of admiration and sadness. This was what true love looked like. When I finally was able to see her, I was sitting in the opposite chair while my uncle, Bob, sat directly next to her.

There were only the two of us in the room as the Neuroscience ICU at the Medical Center only allowed two people at any given time to be in the room.

So I was sitting there watching him hold her hand. He would gently caress her hand with his fingers like dancing along the top of a smooth lake, cautious and attentive not to leave a single ripple.

My uncle was a powerful attorney and good at what he did, but when his princess was lying there in the hospital, he laid his lion's crown aside and his soft side surfaced. Their marriage was the culmination of a lifelong love affair of unselfish admiration and service.

That's what unselfishness can look like in a marriage.

WEDDINGS ARE A GREAT MIRROR TO THE PAST

All marriages start off selfish. And before you say, "Biff! How can you say such a thing? People are madly in love when they first get married. It's after the've been tougher for years and seen each other's dirty laundry that they lose that spark."

Hear me out. Do you remember when you first started dating your spouse? For some of you that may be hard to remember, it's been so long. Congratulations! For others, that may have been last week! Welcome to the party!

No matter when it was that you both said, "I do" and consummated your marriages with vows and intimacy, what were your interests?

What were your hopes and dreams and plans for the future? Think about it for a moment. Try to think back to when you were single and the whole world revolved around you. Even if you think in a romantic way, it's easy to think of these things, right? I bet many of those interests haven't changed.

> I like what you do for me.
> I like the way you make me feel.
> I'm happy when I'm around you.
> You complete me.
> You're an answer to prayer.

I'm sure many of you have uttered these kind of words at some point in your life and marriage. And they sound good, don't they? They're uplifting and showing the other person how much they mean to us. But, what's the common thread in all of those statements?

Me. Me. Me.

I like how *I* feel.
You make *me* feel great.
You make *me* whole.

With all of those things, it's about you, right? And even if it sounds romantic, it's still based in selfishness. Don't get me wrong. These aren't bad comments and I don't want you to feel wrong for saying them. They're good to say to your spouse. I just want to highlight that despite their cheeriness, they're still selfish remarks.

When two selfish people come together, something must give, or they'll be at each other's throats in no time. We see this in far too many marriages, and it's because they haven't killed off their selfish *me* syndrome.

If you want your marriage to last and prosper, you must go from a me-centered mindset to a spouse-centered approach. When you do, your marriage has a substantially higher chance of becoming a forever marriage than if you were to stay self-centered.

And remember, a forever marriage isn't staying married with someone for several decades and not getting divorced, but being with someone that you can't imagine another second without. The kind of marriage that's complete. The kind of marriage that's centered on Christ. The kind of marriage with each other as the focal point. The kind of marriage where you become one.

And so, many times even seemingly unselfish gestures or statements are self-serving. Think about it this way. Let's say that I am being unselfish and I'm thinking about Rhonda's best interest. At the wedding I mentioned earlier, it was raining. And it was a formal wedding, which means I was wearing a tuxedo. And Rhonda wore a long, beautiful formal dress. She was stunning! She was smoking hot.

GENEROSITY IS OFTEN DISGUISED AS SELF-SERVING

Imagine this. I'm at First Baptist in the chapel. You can't park near the chapel, and so I had to park a ways out and we're about to leave to go to Hughes Manor. And so, we've got to drive to Hughes Manor for the reception, which is downtown near Washington Avenue.

And Rhonda goes, "Oh, it's starting to rain!"

It was a little damp on the sidewalk, but I said, "Nah, it'll be fine." So, we go to walk to the truck and we're about halfway. It's just sprinkling. Nothing too alarming. And then suddenly, it was as if someone had unleashed a theme park-sized wave pool onto us. And here I am trying to be chivalrous with my lovely bride and this happens.

What do I do? We're in the middle of nowhere (in the parking lot) and it's dumping buckets onto us. Well, I did what any smart man would do in that situation and thinks he's going to save the day. I bolt off into the downpour and leave Rhonda standing in the middle of puddles in the parking lot.

I only have one thought: get to the car, get to her, save the day. Luckily, someone much smarter than me (my nephew) had come prepared and whipped out his umbrella and held it over Rhonda as I charged through the storm like a wild gorilla, the tail of my tuxedo flapping in the puddles.

Now, usually when this happens, those around you will look at you and go, "Wow, look at him. He's so thoughtful." They may even nudge their own husbands and make a snide remark of, "I wish you would do that for me." And the husband just grunts.

But, here's the problem in this whole scenario. I was selfish. How you might ask? Wasn't I trying to do something nice for Rhonda? Yes, but what was my motivation? To be the hero.

Look at me, I'm the best husband. I ran in the torrential downpour to get the truck for my wife so she wouldn't get as soaked (never mind that I left her alone in the rain). I open the door for her all of the time. I get her flowers. I shower her with praise.

And if I'm not careful, these thoughts will shift from wanting to do well for her to "she needs to start realizing how great I am and doing for me. Doesn't she realize how lucky she is to have me? All of these other women would die to have their husbands be as awesome as I am."

And before you know it your kind gestures and acts of service become a stumbling block to resentment and increased selfishness. We must be careful with our motives. Even our generosity can be self-seeking.

If we're all selfish by nature, how do we fight against it and ensure we're treating our spouses with love, honor, and respect without ulterior motives?

Well, let's go to the best source of wisdom in this area, the Bible. 1 Corinthians 13, the love chapter.

TRUE LOVE IS SACRIFICIAL

Love is patient. Love is kind.
It does not envy. It does not boast. It is not proud.
It does not dishonor others. It is not self-seeking.
It is not easily angered.
It keeps no records of wrongs.
Love does not delight in evil but rejoices with the
    truth.
It always protects. It always trusts.
It always hopes.
It always preserves. Love never fails[1].

TRUE LOVE IS SURRENDER

Do nothing out of selfish ambition or vain conceit,
    but in humility consider others better than
    yourselves. Each of you should look not only to
    your own interests, but also to the interests of
    others[2].

This sounds lovely and we all believe this, but are we doing it?

When I ran to get the truck in the rain, was I doing it sincerely for Rhonda because I love her or for her and others to brag on me?

TRUE LOVE PURSUES OTHERS

No one should seek their own good, but the good of
others[3].

How do we seek the good for others without being selfish? Well,
I'll let you off of the hook a little here. It's impossible to be unselfish to
your spouse and selfish in other areas of your life.

The key to learn here that will enable you to be more selfless is to
think, "How can I be a giver? How can I be a doer? How can I do unto
others in an unselfish way without self-serving, self-centered intentions?"

TRUE LOVE IS WITHOUT DISCORD

From where jealousy and selfish ambition exist, there
will be disorder in every vile practice[4].

The Bible is clear. Wherever there is selfishness there will be
disorder. While selfishness breeds disorder, what does unselfishness
create?

A generous person will prosper; whoever refreshes
others will be refreshed[5].

The more selfish we are, the more chaos and disorder we'll bring.
The more generous you are, the more prosperity you'll bring on
others and yourself.

SURRENDER TO CHRIST

The ultimate act of selflessness is to surrender our lives and our wills
to God, and to let the Holy Spirit create a new creation within us.

But I do not account my life of any value nor as

precious to myself, if only I may finish my course
and the ministry that I received from the Lord
Jesus, to testify to the gospel of the grace of God[6].

Do you count yourself as nothing? This doesn't mean you discount your innate worth. It's only speaking to how you perceive the importance of others in your life. This is total surrender. In order to be unselfish in our marriages, each person must surrender individually to one another.

Every day we wake up, we must kill our alpha mentality. Just like our Great Dane, Daisy. I shared with you earlier, we had to train her to submit to our rule by holding her by all four legs every morning until she stopped fighting and submitted. It is the same for us. We must submit our will to God each day so that His will shines through. Our life is no longer about us, it's about our spouse's needs.

This is why the Apostle Paul spoke so much about surrender. Even our spiritual walk with God is this way. We look to God to provide and supply all of our needs in a selfish way. And yes, God said He will, but again, what are our motives? Are seeking God and praying daily and going to church and studying scripture to truly know God more and to develop an intimate relationship with Him our true motives, or are we only doing that to see what we can get from Him?

THE 4 SCALES TO UNSELFISHNESS IN YOUR MARRIAGE

- *Admit to yourself and to your spouse that you're selfish.*

Not only do you need to realize this, they need to know that you understand it. This makes it real and holds you accountable. Now, understand that you both must realize this.

When your spouse comes to you and says, "I'm a selfish person and I need to work harder each day to serve you like Jesus Christ loved the church."

The other person doesn't need to say, "It's about time you realized that!"

No, this is not healthy and I do not recommend it. Even if it were true, don't do that. Plus, the simple fact is, you're both selfish by nature, so this rings true for everyone.

We're selfish by nature. We all need to realize this. And please don't be sitting there thinking, "Man, I wish my spouse was reading this book. They need to hear this!"

The whole point here is that we're all selfish by nature, but we can overcome it by focusing our thoughts and actions toward the good of our spouses.

YOU CAN CONTROL YOU

Rhonda and I do couples counseling. Oftentimes, the counseling or calls we get are what we call "911 Calls." This is where they're on the brink of divorce, they're separated, someone's being verbally or physically abusive, and immediate action is required.

One of the first traits we look for is selfishness because the only person you can control and change is you. No matter what your relationship looks like with your spouse, you can't control them and you'll never change them. Only God can do that.

The only person you can control and change is yourself. Do you want your spouse to change? You change. Do you want your spouse to admit they're being selfish and to treat you with more honor and respect? Do you admit it and show them the honor and respect you crave.

Here are a few tests you can do to see whether you're being selfish. Let me remind you, all of these selfish tendencies are normal and requires diligence and intentional action to eliminate.

*Have you ignored your spouse's feelings or interests, and
instead, insisted on having your own way?*

I guarantee you that you've done this at some point. And if you
haven't, you will. If you ever said, "I really want this to happen," then
you've fallen into this trap. You may phrase it differently and it may
come off super genuine and kind, but it's still selfish. And your
spouse may say, "We're a team. We should do this instead."

If you're thinking about the betterment of your spouse and their
desires and needs, you're good to go. If it's all for you (primarily or
against their wishes), it's selfish.

This doesn't mean you can't enjoy things, or that if you do, you're
automatically being selfish. You can both be selfless and enjoy things
at the same time. But if you ignore their feelings to get your way,
there's the problem.

Have you made demands or requests?

"But Biff, that's how my parents or grandparents lived back in the
day. Men and women just had their own roles. That's just the way
things were."

*Have you withheld the desires of your spouse or thrown
tantrums when you didn't get your way?*

This is one of the most prevalent ones we've seen in our thirty
plus years counseling and working with married couples. We see this
a lot with women punishing their husbands by refusing sex or the
silent treatment. And the men pouring themselves into their work
and disengaging from the kids. Both are detrimental and childish.

We've seen so many wives who were taught, "If you want to get
your way, withhold sex from him. He'll come around right away." Or,
"If that doesn't work, bombard him with passive aggressive comments
until he runs away or gives you what you want."

That's selfish and childish behavior. It's wrong.

"But Biff, he was being a real jerk. You don't understand the circumstances."

It doesn't matter. Love holds no account of wrongs and does not do things only when they're convenient or deserved. If that were the case, we'd all be alone. The only person you can control is you and how you respond.

The same things applies to men. A man may say, "Well, if she won't have sex with me or if she keeps treating me like garbage, I'll block her from the bank accounts" or "I'll keep this raise and promotion to myself and use it to get my needs met elsewhere."

Wrong. Wrong. Wrong. This is a recipe for disaster on a massive scale, and not just with your family.

BE YOUR SPOUSE'S HELPER

Have you ever listened to yourself on a recording? Do you sound like what you think you sound like? I bet not unless you're an actor or regularly do podcasts. Even then, our recorded voice sounds different than what we hear when we speak.

The same goes for how we act. To be our spouse's helper is to say, "Hey, you're doing this" or "You're doing that" or "You're acting this way." And then for us to be a teammate we say, "I'm sorry. I don't mean to be that way."

It's tough to do this, especially when emotions are running hot.

It's the same when we're being selfish.

"Do you hear how selfish that sounds?"

Now, we got to be careful with how we approach this and bring it to their attention. The goal is not to be selfish, just the reminder.

PRICELESS TREASURE

- *Remember your spouse's incredible value.*

The more you treasure your spouse, the more you will treat them in an unselfish and sacrificial manner.

> For where your treasure is, there your heart will be also[7].

What do you treasure? Do you treasure your spouse? Most people take their spouse for granted. After my Aunt Linda had her stroke, Rhonda and I both said, "Man, we don't want to have regrets." Imagine for one moment, God forbid, the Lord called your spouse home before you got home today. What would you regret?

What would you wish you had said or done?

Would you say, "I wish I would've valued her more. I wish I wouldn't have been selfish in this way or that way. I wish I would've been more loving."

We should never live life with regrets.The way we do this is to remember the incredible value of your spouse and others. Imagine how you would feel without them. Focus and imagine all of the good qualities about them. This will remind you of what you valued in the beginning and will allow you to value them even more in the current time.

Because we are creatures of habit, we get used to a routine which causes us to take all of our blessings for granted. Our spouses usually become the prime victims of this.

- *Learn to make sacrifices.*

Another great reminder on how to be unselfish is to learn how to make sacrifice on a daily constant basis. Sacrifice is the ultimate weapon against selfishness.

> Do not withhold good from those to whom it is due, when it is in your power to act[8].

Unselfishness and sacrifices and giving sacrificially is a big deal. This doesn't just involve money. This includes your time, your talents, your service, your personality and imagination, and your goodwill.

SACRIFICE IS SERVICE IN SECRET

There used to be a widow that lives across the street from us. I used to watch her mow her own lawn. She used a push mower. And despite her having two sons, they were never really around to help her. They were both grown and out of the house by then.

One day when I was mowing our own yard, I thought to myself, "I'm going to sneak over there and mow her yard for her." And I did. And the great thing was, she didn't even see me do it. And then the next week, I did the same thing. I mowed her yard.

And then I did it the next week and the following week after that. The only thing I did was make sure that she either wasn't home or that she wasn't outside at all. And since her house doesn't have windows on the front, this made it a little bit more difficult if she was home. The really awesome thing about this is I was able to do this for over two years without her knowing.

As a matter of fact, the neighbor that lives right beside me came over one time and said, "Hey, are you mowing Miss so-and-so's yard?"

I said, "Why do you ask?"

"Because she came over and accused me of doing it."

I laughed and said, "Yes, it was me. But don't say anything."

Then one day I was outside edging our yard, and I had my headphones in. I was listening to some upbeat rock music. All of a sudden, I noticed something out of the corner of my eye. It was her. She was a quiet lady and had a strange personality. She was just standing there, holding some homemade cookies, she was waiting for me to turn around and shut off the edger.

I pulled out my headphones and asked, "Hey there. What do you need?"

She didn't miss a beat. She said, "I know it's you."

Her words caught me off guard and I didn't know what to say.

"I know you've been the one mowing my yard. My mower doesn't even start."

I just smiled and said, "As long as you live next to me, you will never have to mow your own yard. I'll make sure that it gets done."

Eventually, I ended up hiring some yard guys to do our yard. It freed up my time for other things and prevented severe allergy issues that usually came as a result of mowing the lawn. When they were giving me a quote for their services, I told them to give me a quote that included my yard as well as her yard.

They looked at me strange and then I explained why I was asking. She has since then passed away and I no longer mow her yard. However, the yard guys didn't give me a discount. They claimed it was a package deal. They kept charging the same rate as though they were mowing two yards.

But, here's the point in all of this. I don't say all of this to say, "Oh, look at me! I'm some hotshot and I'm so great." I had more joy out of doing that for her before she found out than I did when she knew. The reason is because it was a sacrifice that wasn't self-serving. In a way, it could have been self-serving because I got a lot of joy out of it, but I wasn't doing it for myself because nobody knew that I was doing it.

When my neighbor found out about it, I didn't want him to know. I didn't want him to say anything to her or tell anybody else that it was me. That is the point when you sacrifice the gift to all is into your spouse. If we can learn to do this in all aspects and areas of our lives, that is what will change the world. That's why when I taught youth years ago, one of the things that I always told them is, "if you have a neighbor, mainly if they're older and they go on vacation, go rake their yard. And if your parents don't mind, set your alarm for 4 o'clock in the morning and go there in the dark before anybody else wakes up. Then come back and go to sleep. Do it during a time when they won't know that you're doing it and they won't know that you did it for them."

Sacrifice and service is an act that does not need reward. It does it without boasting and without fanfare. If we practice sacrificial love like this, make sure that your acts of sacrifice don't turn into acts of selfishness. In other words, if I would have said, "Look at how much I've done for her. I'm amazing." Or, "She owes me." That would be selfish.

YOUR SPOUSE CAN BE YOUR SOUNDBOX

- *Act in humility.*

I love Tony Evans. He says, "A correct way to find humility and to help your marriage is to meet with your spouse for an hour each week and to hear where you've messed up. That'll make you humble."

Your spouse knows you better than anyone does. So give this a try. Go up to your spouse sometime this week and say, "Where'd I mess up this week? What are some ways that I can improve on this week?"

In other words, you're not asking them for some vague overview, but specifics on where you failed and lacked in where you can improve. This will help both people be more humble and servants to the other.

I'll warn you though. This can become a catch 22. Because if you know that the meeting is coming up, or if you're like me and you forget, then you'll want to constantly have this running through your mind so that you have something to share. On the other hand, if you know that this meeting is coming up and your spouse is going to tell you where you've messed up and where you can improve, you may be on your best behavior.

This also plays into the communication that we spoke about

133

earlier. This opens up a pathway for both spouses to be open, transparent, and honest in a safe environment to correct anything that's wrong, and build up what is right.

- *Shelve the **me** syndrome and replace it with **we***.

This is the most critical thing to remember. If you put your spouse first, you can't go wrong. If you spend your entire marriage in life trying to meet your spouse's needs above your own, you will have a blessed and prosperous marriage.

SELFISHNESS IS PRIORITIES OUT OF WHACK

Usually, when we are being selfish, it's because what we are doing or saying is important to us. We think it's the most prevalent thing that must be handled in that moment. But if we take a moment and step back, then we're able to see the whole point and bigger picture of what we're doing and saying. We can then see that we're being selfish.

God has given each of us a certain amount of time in this world. Every day is a blessing. And when we realize this, and no longer matters whether your spouse is being selfish in your marriage. It no longer matters whether your spouse is treating you well or not, whether your wife is being romantic enough, whether your husband is engaged or treating with love and respect.

And when you back off for a second and you look around you, and you see people who are in turmoil because they've lost somebody they loved, it opens your eyes to what really matters. Then you think, "Why am I being so selfish right now?"

It puts things into perspective about what really matters and whether what you're arguing about is even worth the time. Not every battle needs to be one. And not every conversation or argument needs somebody to be right.

One thing that really helps is a mindset of gratitude. I used to think that when you're married you live the same life together. But the reality is, you're not. You still live two separate lives. If you work, and you spend at least eight hours a day living a separate life from your spouse. And if you have a long commute, that's just extra time. She has a separate day from you as well.

It's two separate lives that come together at the end of the day. You may be on the same path, but during the day or at various times of your life, those paths split and go different directions.

Sometimes life might kick you in the face and it's great for her. Other times it might kick her in the face and it's great for you. This is why you are a team. You do life together. When one is weak, the other is strong. When one is down, the other brings them up.

For this reason, you might come home and think, "Man, life is so good." And then she comes home and you feel like she's dragging you down with her mood and pessimistic attitude. And you might think, "If I can just take her out of my life, everything is going to be so much better."

What if, instead, you sat back with a mindset of gratitude, and you looked at the situation from her lens and her perspective? It resets the selfish and innate tendency within each of us to a one of altruism.

UNSELFISHNESS HAS NOTHING TO DO WITH FEELINGS

Being selfless to your spouse and others has nothing to do with how you feel. And it shouldn't. It shouldn't have anything to do with your circumstances or your environment or your situations. It shouldn't have anything to do with whether you had a good day or a bad day, but it does. Our feelings and our emotions often rule our lives and our marriages.

If your role in marriage is,

"I'm going to put my spouse before me at all times no matter the cost. I'm going to think about their feelings when I say and do things no matter how I feel. I am always going to consider them more important and significant than myself."

You will have a forever marriage. This becomes even more difficult and more crucial when you have a bunch of Rugrats running around the house. And still, you must remember that you and your spouse are a team. They need you and you need them. You complement one another. You make each other stronger. You cover each other's weaknesses. And you will change the world together.

Selfishness can ruin a marriage. Selfishness can destroy friendships and families. Selfishness can contaminate and fill the world with darkness. However, unselfishness cures it all. You may have been married for a lifetime, but if you don't have a forever marriage that involves you putting your spouse first above yourself and you can't wait to see them every single day, then you've got work to do.

Commit to seeing the world as your spouse sees the world. Discipline yourself to think of them above yourself and put it into action. A forever marriage requires work, but it's worth every single bit of it.

PRAYER

Father, thank you so much for today. Thank you for your word. Thank you that we don't have to just guess about how we should act or how should be or how we should behave or how we should treat our spouse that you gave it in your word and your direction manual to us. We can see it.

Father, I just pray, even though it's so hard for us as selfish human beings, it's so hard for us to put others first, that you instill into us a heart of service and love.

And Father, you showed us how. You sacrificed your very son for us. Help us to be unselfish and help us to put our spouse first and others first, but help us to cherish and treasure our spouse and to put them first on a regular basis.

Help us every morning to wake up and kill that old self and then put you first and our spouses first as well. I just ask the blessing on each marriage.

Thank you so much for the blessing of this ministry and for everyone reading these words right now. Be with them as they learn how to create a forever marriage and use these principles in their lives.

We love you, Father, and pray all these things in Jesus' name Amen.

UNSELFISHNESS RECAP

- Love is unselfishness in action.
- Remember all of the good you've had together and why you fell in love in the first place.
- Be mindful of the acts that you do and that they are not self-serving.
- Love is sacrificial and covers a multitude of iniquities.
- True love is one of service, sacrifice, and full submitted surrender.
- You are your spouse's greater support system.
- Remember that your spouse is priceless. Selfishness comes as a by-product of priorities out of whack.
- Being unselfish has nothing to do with feelings.

LOVE IN ACTION

- Write down the top five memories that you have of your spouse that made you feel the happiest in your entire life. Write down three things that your spouse absolutely loves and then do them this week.
- MEN: Buy your wife flowers, write her a card that tells her how special she is to you, and surprise her with a date night sometime this week.
- WOMEN: Give your husband a shoulder massage while you tell him specific things you're proud of him for and why he's a good man, and then initiate sex with the lights on.
- TOGETHER: Ask your spouse what you can improve and what they need from you. Then, commit to 30 days eliminating the bad and only doing what they asked no matter how inconvenient or bothersome or pointless it may seem to you.

---

1. 1 Corinthians 13:4-8a NIV
2. Philippians 2:3-4 NIV
3. 1 Corinthians 10:24 NIV
4. James 3:16 NIV
5. Proverbs 11:25 NIV
6. Acts 20:24 ESV
7. Matthew 6:21 NIV
8. Proverbs 3:27 NIV

7

BRING IT ALL TOGETHER

What is the difference between a lifelong marriage and a forever marriage? Do you remember? One lasts a long time and you bear with the other person to not divorce, and the other brings joy, life, fulfillment as you long to be with your spouse every day.

Sometimes we think since God hates divorce that we have to just tough it out and stay in a miserable relationship until we die. That is not what God created marriages for nor what He has in store for you. He created marriages for our enjoyment. Marriage is meant to be incredible and fulfilling and to literally connect and share life with your soulmate. You're not called to labor over your marriage but to enjoy every second of it with the person God made just for you.

Do you believe it's possible to have a forever marriage? I hope by now you're saying, "Yes" with confidence and excitement. And despite marriage being tough at times, you know with certainty that your marriage will thrive and succeed if you follow the five pillars of a forever marriage.

We'll touch on them real quick to remind us what we learned.

IT'S NOT EASY, BUT WORTH IT

Building a forever marriage is not easy, but like anything worth it in life, it's worth the struggle and effort. If you're awesome at your job, you probably had to work hard to improve your skills, your education, your disciplines and work ethic, and put forth effort to succeed at it. That's how things function in our world.

Jeff is one of my lifelong friends and college buddies. The other day he had a heart problem. My son and daughter call him Uncle Jeff because that's how close he is with our family. My daughter, Lindsay, works for a cardiologist and said to us one day, "Uncle Jeff needs to have some work done. He needs Maniscalco to operate on him."

We call him Dr. Mani. If you have a heart problem, you go to Dr. Mani at Memorial Hermann. Let me tell you, this guy is an artist at what he does. What he's able to do with hearts is beautiful.

As it turned out, Jeff went to see Dr. Mani and found out he needed a quadruple bypass surgery to clear out his arteries. At fifty-nine years old, he had to go under the knife to remove the build up in his heart. You should see the scar he has on his chest. It starts from his collar bone and goes all the way down to where the abdomen starts. But what's really amazing about this scar is that it's flawless. It's not jagged or raised or spread out like you might see for other scars from intense surgeries.

And with his age, it's incredible compared to what others in a similar situation look like and had done. Dr. Mani is a pure genius at his craft. But you know how? He didn't just wake up one day and decide he was going to work on hearts, picked up a scalpel, and started cutting people open with perfection.

No, he had to work at it for many, many years to hone his skill, his knowledge, and his craft. He had to go to medical school and all of the rigorous training that comes with open heart surgery. He also didn't just float through school by the seams of his pants and get Cs. He was intentional with the courses he studied to become the best in his field.

Your marriage is the same way. The more you put into it, the more you get out of it. The reverse is also true. The less you put into it, the less you'll get out of it. It's the law of sowing and reaping. You always reap what you sowed, but in a multiplied quantity.

The key is to sow (or put in) the right stuff for your marriage to succeed. We learned that the easiest and surest way to create a forever marriage is to follow the *5 Pillars of a Forever Marriage*.

5 PILLARS OF A FOREVER MARRIAGE

1. Honesty
2. Team
3. Contentment
4. Spirituality
5. Unselfishness

The other day I was playing golf. I was on the twelfth hole when Rhonda called me.

"Hey, do you happen to be at the office?" she asked me.

My office is only about a mile or two from our home. So it's real close.

"No, I'm at the course." "Oh, okay."

"Why?" I asked.

"Well, I'm not feeling well."

Keep in mind she watches our grandson on Tuesdays, and that's what day it was. So, she's not feeling well and is watching our grandson while I'm playing golf.

I said, "I'll be through here in six holes."

She said, "Okay. Well, that's fine. I don't want to stop you."

You know, because what I was doing was really important. Finishing those six holes was so much more crucial than driving home to relieve my spouse so she could lay down and feel better.

Well, we hung up and I played the twelfth hole with my buddy with whom I was playing. And before you judge me, she did tell me it was fine to keep playing.

Here's a tip for you men to remember...

Just because she says you can do something, it's not always in your best interest. Your wife should be top priority all of the time.

Can you guess what happened next? I finished that hole and then told my buddy, "I need to call her back."

'I'm sorry you're not feeling well. I started to tell her to keep the six-month old baby away when she said, "I can barely hold the baby. I just really am sick."

It turned out she was really not doing well, so I told my friend, "Hey, man. I need to cut this short and go home. Rhonda isn't feeling well and sounded like she could really use some help, and she's with our little grandson right now."

I could have finished those six holes in under an hour or hour and a half since there weren't many people on the course that day and it was just myself and my buddy, and I was striping the ball. For you non-golfers, that means I was hitting it well. Something I don't always do.

Instead of playing, which is what I wanted to do and she told me it was fine to do so, I left and went home. How much of a hypocrite would I have been if I had kept playing golf after I had just gotten done teaching on unselfishness in our life group class that past Sunday? I could have justified it both ways, but I went with the best option: my spouse. Even though I was playing with a client and was playing well and she had given me permission to enjoy myself, I thought, "How selfish of me!"

It's little things like this that we must be mindful of each day to determine whether we're putting our spouse before our wants, desires, and needs, or our own. That day when I was playing golf, it reminded me that it's easy to get caught up in the day-to-day things and lose focus on what truly matters: our marriages.

Would Rhonda have been okay if I had kept playing golf? Absolutely. Was it better that I stopped and went home to be with her so she could rest? You better believe it! This is what it means to have a forever marriage, where you implement all five of the pillars each and every day.

Let's recap on each one so we ensure we have that engrained into our minds to execute right away in our lives and marriages.

HONESTY

Honesty in our marriages and our lives merely means you function with integrity. What does integrity look like or mean to you? A simple definition to remember is that it's doing the right thing even when no one knows you're doing it or when no one is watching.

In order to have honesty in your marriage, you must first be an honest person. If you're sitting with your spouse and he goes, "Man, I just cheated this business partner of mine out of a ton of money. And we really benefited from it. Isn't that great, honey? Now we get to go on that big family vacation you've been asking about."

The right response would be, "If he cheated on his business partner, what would he be willing to do with me or our kids? How can I trust him with other areas of our life?"

You know what I mean? It's a slippery slope that never leads to the promised land. It only incurs more misery and problems.

Can I tell you a secret?

You're not an honest person. Your spouse isn't an honest person. And neither am I. We're all born dishonest and we naturally look for ways to benefit ourselves as we go through life. It's our human nature to be selfish. If we lack integrity or are selfish, it's going to be easy to be dishonest in our marriages.

When your spouse asks you a question that you really don't want to answer truthfully or it'll be painful if you give them the right and true answer, sometimes it feels easier to tell a small lie to avoid it. And sometimes, we even think we're doing them a favor and protecting them.

The hardest time to be honest with your spouse is always the first time. Each time after that becomes easier and easier the more you let your integrity slip. You begin to think, "I got away with it that last time, I will again. She'll never know."

I did a class on honesty once many years ago when our life group class at church was smaller and just getting started. I have never received so many calls, texts, and requests for marriage counseling in my life. The reason was because I encouraged each person to go home and be honest with their spouse; totally and completely transparent.

The issue was, they didn't follow the key rules that follow honesty. Honesty is not a time for you to just get something off of your chest so you'll feel better or to make them feel worse. That's not the point; it's disclosing secrets. It's to build up your spouse and to develop a more intimate bond together by fully knowing each other. We'll get into secrets more in a bit.

> Therefore each of you must put off falsehood and
> speak truthfully to your neighbor, for we are all
> members of one body[1].

All throughout Scripture we read about the importance of honesty, integrity, and truth.

> These are the things you are to do: Speak the truth to
> each other, and render true and sound judgment
> in your courts...[2]

If the Bible talks so much about honesty, shouldn't be honest in our marriages?

"Yeah, but it said to others or your neighbor."

Your spouse is your neighbor or someone else, isn't he or she? So that covers them too. God is pleased when we're honest and truthful in our dealings and with each other. He also despises liars.

> The Lord detests lying lips, but he delights in people
> who are trustworthy[3].

God detests someone who lies. Another translation says that lying lips are an abomination to God. There's not much stronger verbiage in scripture for anything else. That's intense and must be a big deal to God.

But what if you say, "Well, look. I lied to her or him about this or about that. And no one will know about tit. It doesn't matter. No one sees it. It doesn't make any difference if she or he knows about it or to anyone."

But I'd caution you. We just read that God says lying lips are an abomination to Him. I don't know about you, but I'd sure like to not be on God's naughty list. Life is much better and simpler when we follow what God says is the best way to do things. And if He said to be trustworthy, you can count on it, that's the thing you should do.

We mentioned how integrity is doing something even when no one sees it or knows about it. Well, think about this. Doesn't God know everything? Isn't He omnipresent and omniscient? He's sovereign. He controls and He knows everything in the entire known and unknown universe.

So, do you think that if you're lying or withholding something that He would know about it? Remember, God sees everything.

> Nothing in all creation is hidden from God's sight.
> Everything is uncovered and laid bare before the
> eyes of him to whom we must give account[4].

No matter who may or may not know what you've done, are doing, or thinking, there's always at least one person who does. God.

Honesty all begins with you. Before you can have an honest marriage as a couple, you must be or become an honest individual. And if you struggle in this area, I challenge you to start today and make a commitment to be hones.

But before you do, there are six rules to follow to ensure that it edifies your spouse and your marriage. It also provides a natural and safe method to be open and honest with each other.

1. Make It Mutual
2. Don't Justify
3. Keep It Tight
4. Check Your Timing
5. Silence Isn't Golden
6. Be Safe Ground

MAKE IT MUTUAL

Sit down with your spouse and say, "I want to be honest with you from now on about everything. And I want you to do the same with me."

Realize that if your spouse shares something with you today at lunch or dinner that this is now your avenue to be honest and open with them too about something you may never have shared before.

DON'T JUSTIFY

Just like I could have easily justified playing those six more holes in golf when Rhonda called to say she was sick and asked me to come home. Even though she said it was fine for me to keep playing and to stay, the right thing to do was go to her and help her, not keep playing. I could have justified either one, but the right choice is always your spouse.

Maybe you say, "There's a reason I'm not honest. I just don't want to hurt him." Or, "The last time I was honest, she's been punishing me for it ever since. I don't want that again."

KEEP IT TIGHT (KIND)

Being honest does not give you permission to unload onto your spouse. Use this simple analogy to help you. If you were sitting in a chair and they had a secret, would you want to know about it? Let your spouse make the decision. Don't just assume you're doing them a favor (most times, it's for your own good you aren't sharing).

It's also worth noting, try not to be aggressive when you share something with your spouse or when you're telling them what's wrong. Also, don't assume and prepare yourself mentally ahead of time for them to get mad and jump down your throat. Give them the benefit of the doubt and not automatically assume they'll attack you. And if you're the receiver, know that your spouse is being vulnerable to trust you by sharing something with you. Show grace, patience, kindness, and love.

CHECK YOUR TIMING

The timing isn't always right depending on what you want to share with your spouse. If you're wanting to discuss finances or financial decisions, it's probably not the best time to have that conversation with your spouse when the kids are running around screaming, they need to eat lunch, nap times are just around the corner, or your spouse is overwhelmed, needs to eat, or is exhausted.

Use common sense when approaching your spouse to discuss something. Just keep in mind, don't use this as an excuse to postpone telling them for a long duration. Just let them know, "Hey, I have something I want to talk with you about when you have fifteen minutes of quiet with no distractions."

SILENCE IS NOT GOLDEN

"I didn't lie. I just didn't tell her."

"I didn't lie. I told her the parts of the story she asked for or needed to know."

"I didn't lie. He never asked me."

"I didn't lie. That stuff happened before I knew him. Why would he need to know about that? It's not who I am anymore."

Be careful you don't justify not sharing something with your spouse because you assume you know what's best for them. Silence is never golden and will lead to other opportunities for dishonest conversation and engagement. If you're able to bend the truth here and there, you'll bend it when it really benefits you in the future.

BE SAFE GROUND

If you and your spouse are willing and committing to being honest with one another, you must realize that each of you must be safe ground for the other or it'll never work. If you jump down your spouse's throat the moment they share something with you that offends you, upsets you, makes you angry, or shocks you, do not attack them. And definitely, do not lord it over them and keep punishing them for it down the road.

The purpose of honesty with your spouse is to build an honest relationship and oneness between the couple. If Rhonda says something to me and it hurts my feelings or angers me, I must not react and punish her on the spot.

"How dare you not tell me this! What's wrong with you? How could you do such a thing? You're not the person I married!"

See what I mean? That's not healthy and will only cause your spouse to lose trust in you and the willingness to be transparent and real with you.

If your spouse tells you something that hits you in the core and you need time to let it download before you just react, let them know. Say, "Thank you for sharing that with me and trusting me enough be honest. I appreciate it. This hurt me though and I need some time to decompress so I don't lash out at you. Can we discuss this more tomorrow?"

Have your mother or grandmother ever told you, "If you can't say something nice, don't say anything at all."

This is partially true with honesty in marriage, in the sense that you want to be mindful and careful with how you react and respond to your spouse. It does not give you a license to not tell the truth or to share only partial truths.

The key is that you're safe ground for them, they're safe ground for you, and both parties are being honest with each other in love and grace.

ARE SECRETS OKAY IN YOUR MARRIAGE?

Depending on where you are in your marriage relationship right now or whether you just had an argument with your spouse about something you shared with them because you were trying to be honest, your response might be different.

The short answer is no. But, here's a better question. If this were you, would you want to know? This doesn't mean, would you want to know something that would hurt you. Rather, if there was a secret, would you want to know what it was?

Of course you would! We all want to know secrets. That's why it's so hard for you to not to tell your wife what you got her for her birthday, or your anniversary, or Christmas! We love sharing and we love knowing.

Secrets are never okay in a forever marriage. I can tell you this, it's much easier to be honest upfront on your terms and choice than for them to find out another way or from someone else. It may be painful and uncomfortable at first, but once you get through the first bit of minutia, you can move on and keep building your marriage.

But you say, "Biff, the last time I told my spouse something, it created a BUNCH of problems! We almost got divorced and she left the house for two weeks. I don't want to go through that again."

Well, maybe that's true or maybe it would have come out anyway. The truth of the matter is, you should be truthful with your spouse and with yourself. The longer you're dishonest, the harder it'll be to share with your spouse and the bigger the backlash that it may cause initially when you do. Don't wait.

So what kind of secrets are not okay in your marriage? Let's go over these quickly.

5 SECRETS NOT OKAY IN YOUR MARRIAGE

1. Past Secrets
2. Sexual Secrets
3. Financial Secrets
4. Health Secrets
5. Relationship Secrets

No, this doesn't include birthdays or anniversaries. We're not trying to be legalistic here, but honest and transparent with ourselves in what the motives for our secrecy is while honoring your spouse and your marriage.

PAST

There should be nothing and no one from your past that your spouse does not know about. There should be no surprises that arise when you go on a vacation, move to a city, or suddenly receive a call with some unexpected news, or a mysterious friend request or message thread.

SEXUAL

This is a big one and usually one of the top three reasons why couples get divorced. Sex is a huge deal with marriages, especially with men. This is an area most churches never talk about because it's become taboo.

"We don't say that word in church."

Ever heard that before? If we can't talk about sex in church, where are we going to learn about it in a safe environment the way God intended it to be done? The reason why most people and churches are uncomfortable talking about sex is because they've been diluted with the world's view of sex and don't know what God says about it.

God created sex for pleasure and procreation. Why else would He have commanded Adam and Eve to multiply the earth and that it was not good for Adam to be alone? So, sex (like money) is not evil, it's how we use it or engage in it that dictates whether it's God's original purpose or sin's.

This goes back to being safe ground for your spouse. If you struggle with lust and pornography then you should go to your spouse and say, "Honey, here's a place I struggle with sexually. Can you help me?"

A lot of times it never gets to that point because the man (or woman) will hint at their problem.

"You know, so-and-so has a problem with lust. I heard he watched porn the other night when their spouse was out of town. When she found out, she got mad. They aren't sleeping in the same room anymore. Can you believe it?"

And then their spouses says in response, "If you ever do something like that, I'm out of here."

Do you think your spouse will open up about a porn or sexual problem and secret if that's your ultimatum? Do you see why it's so vital for the health of a marriage to be safe ground?

Ladies, I'll set you free here for a moment. There have been countless studies that show most men (sometimes it's the woman) have higher testosterone levels and sex drive. No, he's not some sex fiend that always wants to have sex and seems to never get enough or some pervert. And no, if he's staring at you and telling you how good you look it's not just because he wants to have sex, he genuinely thinks you look smoking hot! So, take it as a compliment.

Your husband isn't a sex pervert just because he wants to have sex all of the time—especially if you already did an hour ago. He was created to desire you. Let him.

God made him that way to keep him coming back to you, and God created you as the perfect and safe solution to meet your husband's needs. If your husband is coming after you for sex, that's a good thing. If he stops, it might be time to ask why and be honest with one another.

On the converse, I'll set you free men. If your wife isn't initiating sex, doesn't like talking about it, seems to constantly say, "I'm tired" or "I don't feel like it" or "I'm mad at you" or "can we just do it tomorrow?" this doesn't necessarily mean she doesn't desire you or lacks a sex drive.

(Sometimes a male or female will have a hormonal imbalance that does reduce their sex drive due to lower testosterone levels and higher estrogen levels; in this situation, it's best to see a holistic doctor to see what's going on).

The reality is women don't have the same sex drive as men because they weren't created that way and have lower testosterone levels than we do. Plus, their minds are on totally different things during the day than us. A good rule of thumb is, if you're not having as much sex as you want, do some investigating to see what's going on in your wife's mind.

Warning: You could get lost up there, so make sure you tie yourself off to a tree before delving too deep into the forest. It's nothing you've ever seen before.

Oftentimes, a woman will want to satisfy your sexual needs if she feels loved, cherished, and supported. If your wife stays at home taking care of the kids, she's probably really is TIRED and just wants to finally relax and sleep.

You'd be exhausted too if you were running after the little munchkins all day long, while trying to keep the house clean, doing the laundry, doing the dishes, cooking dinner, all while hoping somewhere in there you'll find time to go to the bathroom or eat a banana. Add on that a needy husband coming home who's chastising you for not wanting to have sex at that very second.

Get the picture?

You see men, your wife needs your help. Just like your wife was created to support you with your needs (not just sexual), you were created to provide and supply her needs. And countless studies have revealed that the primary need of a woman is security. So, if you want more sex, support her. Take the load off of her and help out more.

And before you know it, you'll be the one having to pry her off of you. Don't say you haven't been warned.

FINANCIAL

When you were single, you had separate bank accounts. This is only natural because you didn't know each other yet (or maybe you did) and you were living a singular life on your own. But when you got married, everything joined together.

Just like scripture tells us two become one flesh, you and your spouse became one entity.

"Why should this matter, Biff? We're both working professionals. What's the big deal if I keep my own account and she hers?"

Here's the deal, even if you're both okay with that arrangement, it opens up the door for strongholds to manifest in your marriage. Remember, the first secret leads to the next, and to the next.

Any secrets are not a good thing in marriages. And besides, if you're still thinking, "It's my life and her life," that's not healthy. It's no longer "my life" and "her life" but "our life." You are a couple now. You made the choice to marry your spouse. Therefore, your spouse is now your teammate.

HEALTH

This one could tie into past secrets but I'll keep it separate for now. Do you have any health concerns that run in your family? Were you on medication for a psychological issue? Did you have to get certain vaccinations when you were in the military or traveling abroad? Do you have an STD, HIV, AIDS, or something else?

These are the kind of things your spouse should know about, especially before you get engaged and married. But this isn't just for previous health issues. It's also relevant for ongoing and things that develop in the future.

Are you having problems with your gut? Are you struggling to sleep at night or having the same nightmare time and time again? Do you get the same debilitating migraine at the same time or in the same situations every single day? Your spouse needs to know these things so they can be there for you, not assume you're disengaged or irritable for no reason, and so they don't take offense when you are a bit more exhausted, disinterested, or short with them.

As we grow together, there will be minor and more severe health issues that arise. The key is to be honest with your spouse, be safe ground to discuss it, and work together through it, no matter how minuscule or dire it may appear. If nothing else, this is one of the most crucial times when your spouse will need you most.

If having a cold stinks, just think what it would be like to constantly have a pounding headache, nausea, dizzy, rushing to the bathroom at a moment's notice, find out you have a grapefruit-sized tumor in your abdomen, or breast cancer, or some brain-degrading illness. Not fun.

Be there for one another and honest. If your spouse isn't talking, isn't helping around the house or with the kids, or doesn't want to have sex, it may be because they aren't feeling well, are thinking about something else that's stressing them out or causing concern (even about someone they know that's health-related). Don't assume they hate you or are ignoring you intentionally.

This is why it's even more important to keep an open and honest line of communication.

RELATIONSHIPS

As a financial advisor, I've seen and experienced an array of clients and situations. I have clients who make little, and clients who could buy a private island without blinking an eye. I have young clients just getting out of college and starting their careers and others who have been in the game for well over sixty years. I have single, married, widowed, and divorced alike.

Many of them are widows who need guidance in what to do with the inheritance and their finances when their husbands die. Some are divorces.

I have a widow right now that I engage with on a regular basis. When I have a meeting with her, I tell Rhonda. When my phone is blowing up from messages from her, I tell Rhonda. When I'm going to meet up with her to sign forms or discuss her finances and give her advice (she needs me for everything), I tell Rhonda. Do I need to tell her every time? No, but I do because there's no secrets and it builds trust and accountability.

I had to meet with this same women over five times within a two-week span. If I hadn't kept Rhonda in the loop, she could have asked, "Who are you meeting with so much? Who keeps texting you?" And if she were to find out it's a woman, she could be like, "Why didn't you tell me about this relationship? Is there a reason you didn't tell me?"

And even if there was nothing going on, it's fractured the trust and planted a seed of doubt. Seeds of doubt and lack of trust brood vipers. We don't want any snakes loose in our gardens.

If you're talking to or have to meet with someone of the opposite sex, your spouse should know about it. And, you should not have friends of the opposite sex that you speak to and/or hang out with on a regular basis like you might have when you were single. That's no longer appropriate in a marriage setting.

There should be no secrets of a relational manner in your marriage.

TEAM

We've spoken quite extensively about team. And if you remember, your team is comprised of only you and your spouse. And we touched on how hard it is to realize the reality that our children are not part of that equation. Neither are friends, coworkers, in-laws, or parents.

A good way to think about kids is God leasing them to you for a period of time before sending them off to produce for God's kingdom. It's a great blessing to have children, but they're a momentary assignment and not part of your marriage team.

> That is why a man leaves his father and mother and is
> united to his wife, and they become one flesh[5].

THE SANDWICH SOCIETY

We live in a sandwich generation. Let me explain. If I were to take 50 couples from any given group, I bet you that at some point (if you haven't already) will have a situation where you either support your children, or you've been supported by your parents. This sometimes leads into, "I cannot support them financially, so I'll let them live with us."

On the surface, this is fine. We should support our parents and our children and one another. As it relates to team in marriage, we must keep in mind that none of them has our best interest at heart, only our spouse.

I'll give you a few examples.

Let's say one of your parents dies and the other comes to live with you so you can take care of them, or they get ill, so they move in so you can watch over them. This could lead to problems if you let them dictate what you and your spouse do and if they come in between you and your spouse's team.

A good rule is that if any issues do arise, the spouse who is the child of the parent(s) involved, handles and confronts them. Meaning, if your mother-in-law is overstepping her bounds your marriages and trying to control what you do in your marriage or how you raise your kids, and so forth, her daughter should confront the mom, not you as the son-in-law. And even better option is for that spouse to set the ground rules with their parents before you even get married to where they make it clear, "My spouse and I are a team. If you try to come in between us, I will stand by my husband's side and will choose him every time. Don't make me choose."

There is nothing wrong with doing this and this does not mean you're dishonored or disrespecting your parents. On the contrary, you're showing them a high level of honor and respect by establishing the boundaries and supporting your spouse.

> You must protect your marriage at all costs because the devil will use everything in his arsenal to destroy it and bring division. Kids. In-laws. Parents. Siblings. Finances. Sex. Cursing. Porn. Secrets. Doubts.

You name it, he'll use it.

THE GROUND RULES

These are things like...

"We're good with you moving in with us, but I just want you to know, we will have our time alone and we will work things out between the two of us."

When you're having problems with your spouse, you don't go to your parents and tell them all about it. You keep that private between you and your spouse and work it out together, without outside influence.

Now, this doesn't mean you don't seek help. It just means that if you have someone (like a parent) telling you what you should do with your marriage and talking down about your spouse, that's not okay. What is good and healthy is seeking a counselor, a third party who has the best interest in mind for your marriage.

No matter how much your parents may love you, they will not care about your marriage as much as you will. It's built in them to protect you above all else, even if that means from your spouse.

Just remember, your parents and others are not on your team. They may be support figures and allies, but not the main members of your marital bond. If this is hard to comprehend, then think about it this way.

Would you have sex with them? This sounds weird, but let me explain. Meaning, would you have sex with your parents, your friends, coworkers, or anyone else other than your spouse? If you say,

"No" (and it should be no if you're in a healthy and stable relationship) then it's easy to see that the only person on your team (who you
have sex with) is your spouse.

STRONGER TOGETHER

> Two are better than one, because they have a good
>   return for their labor: If either of them falls down,
>   one can help the other up. But pity anyone who
>   falls and has no one to help them up. Also, if two
>   lie down together, they will keep warm. But how
>   can one keep warm alone? Though one may be
>   overpowered, two can defend themselves. A cord
>   of three strands is not quickly broken[6].

We were not made to do life alone. This is why God created
marriage and joined male and female together as one in marriage.
Lean on your spouse and let them depend on you. Use each other's
strengths for joint gain and cover each other's weaknesses and faults.

Forgive quickly and forget forever. Grudges and old wounds
fester into poisonous pits that only kill the container. Let that stuff go
and move on.

THE 5 C'S TO TEAM

1. Commitment
2. Communication
3. Coordination
4. Consideration
5. Clarity

These five things will help you work as a team. If you're

committed to your spouse, being honest, supportive, and doing whatever it takes to see your marriage succeed, then you'll communicate openly and transparently, you'll coordinate with your spouse to be honest and open together, you'll consider your spouse's needs and desires over your own, and you'll seek clarity to fully know and understand your spouse.

Commitment - You're committed to be honest and selfless with your spouse.

Communication - You speak openly and gently with your spouse, as well as receive them with patience and grace.

Coordination - You understand that timing is a key factor when discussing secrets and things of importance. You make the effort to put your spouse first and make time for one another.

Consideration - You understand it's not all about you, but about your spouse's needs. This is where you put aside self ambition to the betterment of your spouse.

Clarity - You share a linear goal and vision, and both are on the same page.

When you have all five working in harmony, you create something truly special and unique. A forever marriage.

CONTENTMENT

Paul teaches us that discontentment breeds *"constant friction among people who are depraved in mind and deprived of truth"* who *"imagine godless is a means of gain.*[7]*"*

He goes on to elaborate how those who desire to be rich are more prone to temptation and get caught up in deceit and corrupt actions in the pursuit of that gain. He says that the love of money is the root of all evil even though many people misquote that scripture by saying, "money is the root of all evil."

The truth is that our love of something dictates whether it's of God or the sinful flesh. We are to pursue *righteousness, godliness, faith, love, steadfastness, and gentleness*[8].

If we have the love of money then we don't have contentment. Hebrews 13:5-6 tells us to "keep your life free from the love of money, and be content with what you have, for He [the Lord] has said, 'I will never leave you nor forsake you.' For we can confidently say, 'The Lord is my helper; I will not fear; what can man do to me?'"

To be content is merely to be mentally and emotionally satisfied with the way things are and with who you're married to. Here is a quick test you can do at any time to determine whether you're content.

If you say or think, "If I just have that or get that or if this just happened, then I'll be happy."

If you have that thought or notion...I don't dare if it's a raise, a promotion, a bonus, someone else's spouse. It could even be, "If my marriage was like this..."

If you have anything like that go through your mind, discontentment is taking ground. But we learned eight ways to make contentment a habit in our marriage.

8 WAYS TO BE CONTENT IN YOUR MARRIAGE

1. Realize you and your spouse aren't perfect. None of us is perfect, so show each other grace.
2. You can't control your spouse, only yourself. You can't change them, so focus on improving yourself and your spouse will come around.
3. Focus on their strengths and their positives. If you create

what you focus on, why not choose to focus (create) more of their good?

4. Walk in gratitude. It's easy to complain and look at the bad, but there's so much good and blessing around us. Be grateful for where you are and what you have been given.

5. Thrive on your spouse's good points. If you want to be content with your marriage, or anything in life, focus your thoughts and energy on what's good around you and in them. If you want to level up faster, brag about it. It doesn't matter what it is. For example, say, "I love how you cook that bowl of cereal. I could never pour the milk as well as you do." That's funny, but it has the same dramatic and positive impact on your spouse and the way you view them.

6. Eliminate negative and toxic influences. Rhonda and I counseled a young couple and husband was extremely successful at his job but his work environment was toxic for his marriage. So, he quit to save his marriage. He didn't want to because it paid well and he was really GOOD at it, but he did it for his spouse, and he knew that if he stayed there, that negative influence would contaminate his marriage and ruin it. Now their marriage is thriving.

7. Spend time in prayer for your spouse and over your marriage. Pray and ask God to bless your marriage and ask Him to give you all of the things we've discussed in this book: honesty, team, contentment, spirituality, unselfishness.

8. Count your blessings in marriage and don't take them (and your spouse) for granted.

SPIRITUALITY

There's a dividing gap between the impact going to church has on your marriage versus being spiritual in your marriage. Going to church is not enough because studies have already shown that the divorce rate is roughly the same for those in the church and out.

This is because many people have made church a consumer sport. They go sometimes on Sundays to get their spiritual fix and then stop going or don't implement what they learned or pursue God on a regularly basis to know Him more. They lack a solid spiritual foundation in themselves, and as a result, their marriage suffers. We must connect with our spouses on a spiritual level.

Jesus tells us in Matthew 18:20 that where two or three gather (come together) in His name, He's there with them. And He goes on to say that we should seek first His kingdom and His righteousness and everything you need (food, water, clothing, protection, favor, blessing) will be given to you[9].

There is no question spirituality is necessary and beneficial in an individual's life; it's equally valuable for a marriage.

SPIRITUALITY REMINDERS

Church — Go to church to be with other likeminded believers who want their marriages to thrive. Encourage others.

There have been many times when I'd say, "Do you want to go to church this morning?" Hoping that Rhonda would say, "No." She never did. She'd say, "Yes, we should."

And on the rare occasion she was tired or not feeling well, she'd ask me, "I'm really tired. Maybe we should just stay home tomorrow." And I'd say, "No, I think e should get up and go."

That's how marriages should work. You build each other up and encourage one another. I'm not saying going to church is the magic pill (we've already seen how the divorce rate is basically unfazed by it) but it definitely helps create that vital spiritual element we each need. Once you say, "No" once to going to church, it begins to lose its priority in your life.

With anything in life, we need accountability and that's what community at church does for you.

Pray — If you don't pray with your spouse, start today. It may feel strange, foreign, or uncomfortable for many of you if you've never prayed together before, or if you rarely pray yourself, but trust me, it'll be awesome!

And if you don't feel like praying but know it's important, then ask your spouse, "Hey, would you mind saying a quick prayer over dinner for us?"

If you're unsure what to say, use this prayer as a template for your future prayers, "Thank you, Jesus, for this food. Thank you for my beautiful spouse and the blessing she is in my life. Thank you for our children and for giving us these precious treasures to mold into your glory. Equip us with your power and love to have a great day today. In Jesus' name. Amen."

Spiritual Conversation — Spend time with your spouse talking about and discussing spiritual things. Share what God is doing in your life, how He's been convicting and challenging you in a certain area, and where your walk with Christ is headed.

We get so caught up in the day-to-day activities and forget to engage in conversations that build us, challenge us, equip us, empower us, and give us true life. Instead of saying, "Well, little Johnny today had his firs poop in the big boy potty. You should have seen how excited he was."

That's good and you should talk about your children and your day, but try to go deeper beyond that and not dwell too long, or only, on trivial things. Don't make them your entire conversation. Before you know it, when you finally go on that date night together, you won't know what to talk about but your kids.

Here's some tips:

Share what God is doing in your life.
Ask what God is saying to them or doing in their life.
Talk about what you'd like to achieve together.

Spiritual Marriage — Think about the Holy Spirit indwelling in your marriage through you and how you treat and love and show respect to your spouse. Think about your life in your marriage and how God can move in it and create something magnificent

UNSELFISHNESS

Marriage is the joining together of two innately selfish beings. If you want to succeed in life and your marriage, you must transition from a self-centered and self-preserving mindset and belief system to one of outward and external giving and generosity. You must become "US-centered."

If you need a fresh reminder, go read 1 Corinthians 13, the love chapter. It'll remind you what love is, does, and looks like. One key ingredient is it doesn't insist on its own way and is not resentful. Are you able to go a day or a week without thinking something negative about your spouse?

If you're up for a challenge, go one week with only doing the things your spouse wants and only showering them with praise and positive affirmations despite whether they or the situation is contrary to that and see what happens. This will teach you (and show them) what it looks like and what it means to do nothing from selfish ambition or conceit, but in humility to count others [your spouse] as more significant than yourself[10].

When you make a conscious decision to put your spouse above

your own needs, it creates new synapses in your brain. You're literally creating new connections in your brain and evolving into a higher being. You should always seek the good of your spouse more than anything else[11]. And in truth, since you're both a team anyway, when you put your spouse's needs first, you actually help yourself.

4 HACKS TO DEVELOP AN UNSELFISH MENTALITY

- **Admit to yourself and to your spouse that you're selfish.**

Literally say to your spouse, "Honey, I'm selfish and I know it." This is not a time for you to agree with them, but to agree that you are too, and then remember your spouse's incredible value and worth.

It's common nature to be selfish, and easier to do when I'm not thinking of the value of my spouse or of others.

- **Learn to make sacrifices.**

Do things for your spouse and give up the things you prefer. Give yourself over to them completely. Is there something they want to do that you really don't enjoy? Do it anyway and do it with a good attitude.

Here's a really good example, the next time your spouse says, "I need to run to the store, do you want to go with me?" and you don't feel like it, go. Better yet, go for them.

The reality is they aren't asking because they need your help (unless the kids are involved), but because they want to spend time with you. And if you go *for* them, that's a double win.

- **Act in humility.**

When we think about the needs of our spouse above our own, we humble our motives and attitude to the glory of our spouses and raise them up. It takes humility to serve others. It takes humility to put aside past feelings, hurts, doubts, fears, or wrongs. It takes humility to say, "I will treat you with honor and respect and love no matter what you do to me. You are my team."

If you both pursue humility, you'll be receptive to instruction, guidance, and hearing the voice of God. And when you start hearing God and doing what He says, miraculous things occur. Just wait and see!

- **Commit to meeting your spouse's needs FIRST.**

Before you can commit to meeting your spouse's needs, you must know what they are. A good place to start is the 5 Love Languages test. It'll break down where you and your spouse show and receive love the best. Don't be surprised if you're both on polar opposites. That's what we want!

And from there, use what we've taught in this book to show your spouse that you love them by meeting their needs. The beautiful thing that you'll discover is that when you focus on satisfying and providing for their needs above your own, they actually reciprocate.

PUT YOUR FOREVER MARRIAGE IN ACTION

These five pillars to a forever marriage are not laborious. They will remove the struggles out of your life and your marriage. They will enrich every aspect of your being, your marriage, your children, your work, your relationships, and your life.

You were put together with your spouse in marriage to be a blessing to others and to each other. If you focus your time and energy and thoughts on serving your spouse, you'll forget anything that you might have disliked, and they'll shine ever brighter to you.

PRAYER

Father, thank you so much for each of these marriages and spouses reading these words.

Thank you for each marriage that is represented here today.

Thank you for them pursuing growth, knowledge, and wisdom to enhance their marriages and make their spouses feel like the true priceless treasure that they are.

I ask for and release a special blessing in the power and the name of the Holy Spirit over every person in the sight of these words that you bless their marriage with supernatural favor and blessing and provision.

Empower them to walk in love and humility and in your power to grow close with you.

Thank you for blessing Rhonda and me with a forever marriage and the opportunity to share our experiences and struggles with the next generations so they can bypass those hurdles and get right to the forever marriage part.

I ask for you to encourage and equip each person with this new mentality and pursuit to change themselves, and fully embody what it means to be a selfless giver for their spouse.

We love you, Father. And we ask and pray all of these things in Jesus' name. Amen.

FOREVER MARRIAGE IN ACTION

- Pick one thing you learned that really stood out to you in this book and focus on doing ONLY that for the next 7 days. Write down each day the results of what you're doing.
- When those 7 days conclude, continue doing that one thing, and add a second one for the next seven days. Write down each day the results of what you're doing. Do this for 30 days and watch your spouse blossom and flourish.

---

1. Ephesians 4:25 NIV
2. Zechariah 8:16 NIV
3. Proverbs 12:22 NIV
4. Hebrews 4:13 NIV
5. Genesis 2:24 NIV
6. Ecclesiastes 4:9-12 NIV
7. 1 Timothy 6:5 NIV
8. 1 Timothy 6:11 NIV
9. Matthew 6:33
10. Philippians 2:3
11. 1 Corinthians 10:24

SHARE YOUR BREAKTHROUGH!

Thank you so much for reading this book and congratulations! You are one step closer to your Forever Marriage and I cannot be more excited and proud of you.

You've shown me that you care about your spouse and your marriage matters to you. Now, it's time to implement what you learned and see your marriage rocket to great heights.

Before you go, I have one last challenge for you that'll solidify what you learned, build the accountability that you need to succeed and see this through, and will help someone else do the same.

Tell me, what was your biggest "Ah-Ha!" moment or breakthrough while reading this book? What stopped you and made you think, "I've never considered that." Or, "That makes total sense."

I'd love to hear how this book opened your eyes to how you can have a forever marriage with your spouse and some practical ways you can start today.

Share your biggest breakthrough or "Ah-Ha!" moment by leaving a review. Your words will touch someone's life and may be the one thing that encourages someone and gives them hope to fight for their marriage.

If you'd like more resources to create a forever marriage and connect with other likeminded couples pursuing God, each other, and raising the marriage success rate, you can join us in our **Soul Mates Facebook Group** to keep growing the Word and your Forever Marriage.

See you there!

SPECIAL THANKS

I would like to acknowledge my parents, who at the writing of this book, have celebrated 62 years of marriage.

Being able to watch their love for one another, no matter the situation, has given me an incredible example to follow.

My mother's love for the scripture has also implanted in me a basis for the biblical truths when writing marriage books and counseling couples.

MEET BIFF ADAM

B. F. (Biff) Adam, III is a native of the Houston, Texas area.

He has been an independent financial advisor for over 35 years and Marriage Counselor with his wife, Rhonda.

Biff is married to his childhood sweetheart, Rhonda, and have celebrated 35 years of marriage.

He has two children with beautiful marriages and three grandsons.

His hobbies include golf, cars, and grandsons.
He and Rhonda spend a great amount of time in their ministry, Soul-mates Ministries, writing books and working with couples in enriching their marriages.

They also teach a bible study "life group" class at Champion Forest Baptist Church in Spring, Texas, for married couples seeking to create a forever marriage doing it God's way.

ALSO BY BIFF ADAM

Forever Marriage Series

Forever Marriage

A Marriage Set Free Series

5 Fundamental Truths About Marriage

5 Myths That Destroy Your Marriage

12 Dangers That Will Damage Your Marriage